Praise for Dutch Oven Cookout

"At last, the book that is going [...] [...]ns (including my seven) back in busi[...] [...]d my Dutch ovens away, along co[...] [...] to show a non-cooking person like [...] [...]s) work! This book is way, way overdue, but it [...] [...]oo late—this is a marvelous manual that must come with every Dutch oven sold!"

DON ASLETT, cleaning expert, businessman, and bestselling author of *Is There Life After Housework* and *Clutter's Last Stand*

"If you are working with youth, the best thing you can do is let them learn to Dutch oven cook in small groups using small Dutch ovens. This book is the best source that I know of for simple, easy recipes for the beginning Dutch oven cook."

DIAN THOMAS, professional speaker, TV personality, *New York Times* bestselling author of *Roughing It Easy*

"Michele has taken all of the fear and confusion out of Dutch oven camp cooking! These recipes and methods are streamlined and simplified so that you can have delicious, filling meals and get on with the day's activities! Whether you're cooking for a family of 3–4 campers, or a big group, these recipes will scale easily. In preparing this book, Michele has really gone the extra mile so you don't have to!"

MARK HANSEN, author of *Best of the Black Pot*, *Black Pot for Beginners*, and marksblackpot.com

"Finally, a guide for even the most novice of Dutch oven chefs. As a seasoned youth camp leader, *Dutch Oven Cookout: Step by Step* is the step-by-step manual I've always needed. A perfect resource for any camp."

STEPHANIE WORLTON, author of *Everything You Need to Know About Girls Camp*

DUTCH OVEN cookout

· STEP BY STEP ·

MICHELE PIKA NIELSON

HOBBLE CREEK PRESS
An Imprint of Cedar Fort, Inc.
Springville, Utah

ISBN 13: 978-1-4621-1134-3

LIBRARY OF CONGRESS CATALOGING-IN-PUBLICATION DATA

Nielson, Michele Pika, 1967- author.
Dutch oven cookout : step-by-step / Michele Pika Nielson.
  pages cm
Includes index.
Summary: Simple, no-fail method of Dutch oven cooking for beginners.
ISBN 978-1-4621-1134-3 (alk. paper)
1. Dutch oven cooking. I. Title.

TX840.D88N54 2013
641.5'89--dc23

        2013002266

Published by Hobble Creek Press, an imprint of Cedar Fort, Inc.
2373 W. 700 S., Springville, UT 84663
Distributed by Cedar Fort, Inc., www.cedarfort.com

Cover and interior design by Erica Dixon
Cover design © 2013 Lyle Mortimer
Interior illustrations by Rebecca J. Greenwood
Photos by Michele Pika Nielson
Edited and typeset by Emily S. Chambers

Printed in the United States of America

10 9 8 7 6 5 4 3 2 1

Contents

INTRODUCTION	**1**
QUICK-START GUIDE	**9**
SECTION 1: GETTING READY	**13**
SECTION 2: THE COOKOUT STEPS	**21**
Important Reminders	**22**
Step 1: Setup	**23**
Step 2: Light	**25**
Step 3: Preheat & Season	**27**
Step 4: Fry/Simmer	**29**
Step 5: Bake	**31**
Step 6: Extinguish & Eat	**33**
Step 7: Clean	**35**
In Case of Rain	**38**

VI

CONTENTS

SECTION 3: THE RECIPES **39**

How to Use the Recipes **40**

Planning Your Menu **42**

Standard Ingredient List **44**

Super-Easy Recipes **49**

Easy Recipes **61**

Intermediate Recipes **73**

SECTION 4: THE WHYS BEHIND THE HOWS **89**

Dutch Ovens **93**

Dutch Oven Kit **121**

Cookout Food **131**

Charcoal & Other Fuel **149**

Planning for Groups **180**

CONCLUSION **191**

LIST OF FAQS **193**

INDEX **197**

ABOUT THE AUTHOR **201**

Introduction

The first time I had really great food out of a Dutch oven, I thought, "This is fantastic! I want to learn to do this!" Dutch oven cooking can be practical and versatile. It can be delicious and unique. But without a good method for how to do it, it can also be frustrating and disastrous. I have talked to many people who have cooked in their Dutch ovens once or twice and then put them away. I don't know all the reasons that so many Dutch ovens end up in the basement or garage for decades, but I personally think it has to do with the frustration level that comes when one doesn't quite know how something works—the same type of frustration you feel when you get a new phone or other electronic device and you just don't know how to make it do what you want it to do.

MY STORY

My journey with Dutch oven cooking began one summer when I had really great Dutch oven food at an outdoor event I attended while visiting my sister in Idaho. (Isn't it interesting that one keeps memories of places where one had really outstanding food? My parents still remember the best French onion soup they ever had; it was in New York, over fifty years ago.) Sometime after that, when I was sixteen, my church congregation planned a several-day camping trip for the teenage girls in my area. No one, including the leaders, knew how to Dutch oven cook, but everyone agreed that it was a good idea to do at least one Dutch oven meal on our trip. Since I was the only one who had relatives who had experience with Dutch oven cooking, the job of figuring it out was delegated to me! I bought some books, made some phone calls, and started learning. My cooking group was borrowing a Dutch oven from a local Scout leader, but he had been storing it in his garage, and it had been sitting with water in it for some time. Thus, my first personal encounter with a Dutch oven involved getting a deep, flaky layer of rust off and getting it "seasoned" and ready to go. As it ended up, the meal I was in charge of turned out well, and the award I was given at the end of the week included the somewhat surprised statement that I had done my Dutch oven meal as planned . . . "And It Worked!"

Over the next few years, I became fairly proficient at Dutch oven cooking, mostly through trial and error and through learning what I could from a few people I knew who did Dutch oven cooking. The next step came when, in my early twenties, I was hired to work at a girls' camp. Each week on cookout day, my job was to have all of the cookout equipment ready to go and help do the cooking. At these cookouts, we had nearly two hundred campers cooking out at the same time. Week in and week out for eight weeks of the summer, every cookout turned out basically the same—burned food, hungry campers, and frustrated, exhausted staff.

Three years later I was back working at the camp again—this

time as the head cook. The camp had just acquired more than fifty small eight-inch (two-quart) Dutch ovens with the idea that with so many small Dutch ovens, the campers could have a hands-on experience, there would be more food to go around, and the whole situation would be better. My first job as cook was to season all the new Dutch ovens and then come up with recipes that could be done in them. The recipes would need to be easy, and each group would need the right tools for preparing the food and maintaining the Dutch ovens. Since there were so many campers, there would need to be written instructions. There would have to be a way to accommodate campers with allergies or special dietary needs. And the food would need to be done quickly so the campers could get on to their other scheduled activities.

During that summer, and many summers that would follow, I went to dozens of cookouts and observed what worked and what didn't. Over time, I fine-tuned my idea of what makes a camp cookout go well. I felt it needed the following features:

★**IT SHOULD BE SAFE.** If the twelve-year-old campers were going to cook their own food, I wanted procedures in place that would keep them safe while still providing them a hands-on learning experience.

★**IT SHOULD BE EASY.** Before I worked at the camp I had been to many cookouts where the experienced Dutch oven cook did all the cooking. I wanted to find a way to cook that was so straightforward a twelve-year-old could do it, and do it without help.

★**IT SHOULD TAKE LESS THAN TWO HOURS.** In the camp setting, everyone was on a schedule. If a cookout took too long, those campers would miss out on another activity.

★ **IT SHOULD MEET FOOD SAFETY REQUIREMENTS.** Early on in my testing process, I heard about too many cookouts where "pink chicken casserole" was served—not what I had in mind when I planned the menu. I wanted to find a way to ensure that meats would get thoroughly cooked, that the cooking pots would be sanitary, and that other food safety principles could be easily practiced.

★ **MAINTAINING THE DUTCH OVENS SHOULD BE PART OF THE PROCESS.** With over fifty Dutch ovens, I knew it would not be possible for the staff to keep the Dutch ovens in good shape—that would have to be done by the campers during the cookout *and* while still meeting all the other criteria.

MAKING PROGRESS

In a process that lasted over ten years, I gradually developed the methods and recipes in this book. As I found ways to do things, I wrote up the instructions in booklet form and sent them out to the cookouts for the campers and staff to use. I collected data, and, every few years, revised the booklet. During the winter I tested recipes at home and then had the campers try them out. Over time, the method became easier to follow and more streamlined.

After several years, we settled into a pattern in which each group of fifteen campers would receive five Dutch ovens and the ingredients for five different recipes. The counselor would divide the campers into groups of three, with each cooking group getting their own bag of charcoal, bag of food, Dutch oven, and booklet. Each counselor had a tool kit that we called a Dutch Oven Kit. It contained the tools and utensils the group needed—tongs for moving coals, cooking spoons, a can opener, and so on. When the food was done, the various dishes were shared among all of the campers in any given group. This meant there were five main dishes to choose from, which made it much easier to accommodate special food needs and picky eaters. Everything still wasn't perfect, but it was much better—the cookouts were less stressful, the campers did most of the cooking themselves, the food hardly ever burned, and (most of the time) the campers got full and enjoyed the cookout.

DELVING INTO THE SCIENCE: THE WHYS AND HOWS

Along with developing recipes in the winter, I also spent time trying to uncover the science behind the process. I wanted to know things like "What happens at a molecular level when you create a seasoning coat on cast iron?" "What is the most efficient way to light charcoal?" and "What type of heat transfer is going on in the food as it cooks?" It seemed to me that if I wanted to make the process better, I would need to understand exactly how things worked and why they worked or didn't work. In my life I am blessed to be surrounded by family members and many friends who are experts in fields such as physics, chemistry, and thermodynamics. As I played with the method, I would ask myself the types of questions listed above, observe what I saw happening, formulate a hypothesis, and then run my ideas by the various scientists in my life. Once we had come up with some good theories, I would try to think of ways to test those theories.

During this time, I also read or reread every Dutch oven book I could find. Most of what I read raised more questions in my mind. One of the biggest questions I had was "What exactly is a seasoning coat?" Much of the information I read was conflicting. After quite a lot of research, I found out. (See "The Physical Chemistry of 'Seasoning'" below.) Knowing what a seasoning coat was from a scientific perspective, helped me know how to improve the seasoning on my Dutch ovens, and helped me improve the step-by-step process I was developing. I did many different kinds of experiments, and my tests led to other discoveries about the hows and whys of Dutch oven cooking. As I continued to learn, I incorporated new tips and instructions into the step-by-step instructions as they now appear in section 2 of this book.

Today, I'm still researching and learning. A few months ago, I realized some specific things about charcoal use I still didn't

THE PHYSICAL CHEMISTRY OF "SEASONING"

So when you "season" your Dutch oven, you apply oil and heat, then the oil magically converts itself into a nonstick coating! What is at work here? It is a process known as cross-linking. The long chains of the oil molecules cross over each other and form new bonds. These bonds change the physical properties of the oil. With the application of the right amount of heat, a hard, glassy substance is formed—the nonstick seasoning coat. Put another way, the fatty acid chains on the triglyceride molecules reconfigure to form a cross-linked polymer network.

understand as well as I wanted to. Again, I found that the information I read elsewhere just raised more questions in my mind. I consulted with scientists and engineers among my family and friends, devised some new experiments, and ended up with some exciting new information to pass on to you in this book!

I'm sure this process won't stop just because this book is going to press. I will continue to do research and will share it through my blog. I hope that as you use this method and read my explanations, you will think of questions and do some experiments of your own. When you do, I hope you will share them with me and others on my Facebook page (Dutch Oven Cookout) or through my website (www .MichelePikaNielson.com).

The cookout steps (section 2) are the most important part of this book. The steps are: 1) Setup; 2) Light; 3) Preheat & Season; 4) Fry/Simmer; 5) Bake; 6) Extinguish & Eat; and 7) Clean.

WHAT IT'S ALL FOR

My goal in writing this book (and getting it published) is to take the frustration out of Dutch oven cooking and make it accessible to anyone who wants to learn. I think that being out in nature—whether in the wilds or in your own backyard—has value. When cooking outdoors is easy, it is that much easier to spend time in nature—by yourself, with your family, or with a group. Spending time in nature can build confidence in children and youth. It can bring serenity and peace to adults. And I believe it can bring anyone closer to his or her creator.

Michele Pika Nielson
Salt Lake City, Utah

Quick-Start Guide

If you are reading this book, you probably fall into one of the following categories:

A. You have never done Dutch oven cooking (or not for a long time) and want to learn.

B. You are an experienced Dutch oven cook and like to read new Dutch oven books.

C. You are someone who is looking for easy recipes.

IF YOU FALL INTO CATEGORY C, I recommend starting with section 3: "The Recipes." Once you have looked through the recipes though, don't neglect to read section 1 and section 2. The information in these sections will help you understand the recipe instructions. You may also want to read part or all of the food topic in section 4.

IF YOU ARE AN EXPERIENCED DUTCH OVEN COOK, you might want to start with section 4. You will find information here that will confirm your suspicions, support your own good discoveries, and demystify things you might have wondered about. Alternatively, you could start with section 2: "The Steps."

IF YOU FALL INTO CATEGORY A, I recommend jumping right in and doing some cooking! It doesn't take long; in fact, you could be eating Dutch oven food several hours from right now! If that appeals to you, follow the instructions below, make your first meal, and then come back and read more of the book.

Here's what you do:

1. BUY OR BORROW A DUTCH OVEN. You can read more information about buying in section 1, page 14, and lots more information about it in section 4, pages 93–95. If you already have a Dutch oven, but you aren't sure if it's ready to use, you can read all about "Dutch oven rehab" on pages 96–99.

2. PICK A RECIPE. I recommend starting with Cheesy Chicken, an easy favorite. Turn to page 50 and make a shopping list for ingredients to fit the size of Dutch oven you have or plan to purchase or borrow. Don't forget to put charcoal on your list—I would plan on buying a small four-pound bag of Matchlight— this should cover your needs this first time.

3. GATHER UP SOME BASIC TOOLS. You may eventually want to make yourself a Dutch Oven Kit as suggested in section 1 (page 15), but for your first cookout, you just need a few things you probably have around the house:

- matches or a lighter
- a roll of foil
- a few paper towels
- a non-metal cooking spoon or spatula

- a can opener
- a hammer with a claw
- vegetable oil—any kind
- a jug of water
- some metal tongs

4. GO SHOPPING. Buy your recipe ingredients, charcoal, and anything from the above list that you couldn't find around the house. Buy a Dutch oven if you need one. If you plan to purchase an eight-inch Dutch oven, as I recommend, it is smart to call the store before you go to make sure they have one. I have had good luck finding eight-inch Dutch ovens for a good price at farming supply stores.

5. FIGURE OUT WHERE YOU WILL COOK. Take everything you have purchased and gathered to that location. For this first cookout, I suggest doing your cookout outdoors at home. All you need is a driveway, a cement or paving stone patio, a cement front porch, or an area with hard-packed dirt. If you live in an apartment and don't have an area like this available, find a friend who does or go to a nearby park that has an area designated for grilling.

6. OPEN YOUR BOOK TO SECTION 2 (page 21). Work through Steps 1–6. When you get to *Step 4*, refer to the recipe for Cheesy Chicken, page 50. In *Step 6*, use the soup can method to extinguish your coals—see FAQs on page 34. This part will take a little over an hour.

7. TIME TO EAT. Yum!

8. AFTER YOU EAT, take your Dutch oven inside and wash it in your sink. You can wash your Dutch oven with mild dish soap and hot water like any other pot that you would hand-wash. Dry your Dutch oven with paper towels. At future cookouts, you can clean your Dutch oven at your cookout site, but for your first cookout, cleaning it inside can make the process easier. Don't be alarmed if a little rust appears on your Dutch oven after you clean it. This will go away the next time you use it.

9. CALL OR TEXT YOUR FRIENDS to say, "I just did my first cookout!"

SECTION 1:
Getting Ready

1. DUTCH OVEN   14   5. FUEL   17

2. DUTCH OVEN KIT   15   6. EXTINGUISHING CAN   18

3. FOOD   16   7. A PLAN   19

4. WATER   17

What You Need for Your Cookout: 1) Dutch Oven; 2) Dutch Oven Kit; 3) Food; 4) Water; 5) Fuel; 6) Extinguishing Can; 7) A Plan

Before you go on your first cookout, you will need the items shown on the previous page (or something like them). Below is some brief information about each item. For more details, please see section 4.

1. DUTCH OVEN

Most people I talk to who want to learn how to cook in a Dutch oven fit into one of these categories:

★   They own a Dutch oven, but it is still new in the box.

★   They have a Dutch oven but haven't looked at it in years.

★   They don't own a Dutch oven but might want to get one.

If you have a new Dutch oven, it may be preseasoned. Check the box or tag; if it says "preseasoned," all you need to do before you cook in it is rinse it with a little hot water and dry it out. If it doesn't say "preseasoned" anywhere, it probably isn't and you will need to season it before you cook in it. First-time seasoning isn't hard, and there are several methods to choose from so you can pick the one most convenient for you. Please see "First-Time Seasoning Methods" on page 101.

If your Dutch oven has been sitting around, it may need some TLC before you use it. The flowchart on page 96 will help you decide what kind of care it needs.

If you have not purchased a Dutch oven but are thinking about getting one, I recommend starting small. The eight-inch (two-quart) size is a great size for beginners—it doesn't take much storage space, is easy to handle (not as heavy as the bigger sizes), and can be useful in your indoor kitchen even if you don't plan to use it often outdoors. There is also less risk involved in making a recipe for the first time in an eight-inch since it only holds four to five servings. Even if you decide to get a larger one later, your small one will always come in handy. You can read more about how to choose one to buy starting on page 93 and on pages 106–108

2. DUTCH OVEN KIT

Having a "Dutch Oven Kit" makes it so that you can grab and go when you are ready to cook out. A Dutch Oven Kit contains the items you need to follow the steps—a hammer to use as a lid-lifter, a can opener, matches, and other essential items. As you start experimenting with Dutch oven cooking, I recommend gathering the items in the list below. You may be able to find most items already at home, but I recommend doing some bargain shopping to get a second of each item so that you can keep them in your kit. It makes getting ready to cook out so much simpler, especially if you are cooking out away from home. For more detailed descriptions of each of these items, please see "Making Your Own Dutch Oven Kit" on page 121.

ESSENTIAL DUTCH OVEN KIT INVENTORY

- hammer/lid-lifter
- leather gloves
- long metal tongs
- foil
- matches or lighter
- vegetable oil
- paper towels
- cooking spoons (plastic or nylon)

- can opener
- paring knife
- salt & pepper
- ash brush
- plastic pot scraper
- biodegradable soap
- soft fir or spruce cones (for cleaning)
- garbage bags

SECTION 1: *Getting Ready*

3. FOOD

In combination with the method, the recipes in this book are designed to

★ be easy to take camping

★ be nearly impossible to burn

★ be made in several standard Dutch oven sizes

★ guarantee that the meat gets cooked to safe temperatures

★ use no dishes other than the Dutch oven

★ require very little knife use

★ include gluten-free and vegetarian options

★ be as foolproof as possible

I designed the recipes with kids and youth in mind—but they are a good jumping-off place for adults as well.

When I'm getting ready to cook out, even on my own porch, I like to put all the canned and dry goods for a certain recipe in a paper sack with a copy of the recipe. I also measure and package up any refrigerated and frozen ingredients. Before I leave, I pull the items I need out of the fridge and freezer and put them in the sack. I then double-check the items in the sack with the ingredients on the recipe to make sure everything is there. If I am going camping and need to keep the refrigerated and frozen items cold, I label them, pack them in my cooler, and then add them to the paper sack at my campsite. Premeasuring and bagging your ingredients is especially helpful if you are cooking out with kids or with a large group.

For more information on the food and recipes in this book,

please see: "How to Use the Recipes," page 40; section 4: "Cookout Food," page 131; and "Planning for Groups," page 180.

The recipes in this book can also be made indoors—with or without a Dutch oven. Making a recipe indoors before you go camping can help you feel more at ease when you first make it outdoors. For more information, see pages 135–138.

4. WATER

Water is used as an ingredient in many of the recipes. It is also used in *Step 7: Clean*. Please note that cleaning your Dutch oven with water will not damage it, as long as you follow the steps carefully. (For more information, see "Dutch Ovens—Cleaning FAQs," page 115.) I usually carry water to my cookout location in a jug like the one shown in the photo.

5. FUEL

To follow the Cookout Steps, you will need charcoal briquettes that

1. are high quality (don't go for the store brand—they don't work as well)

2. weigh around one ounce each (don't go for "extra large")

3. are pretreated (for example, Matchlight)

You can make your own pretreated briquettes using regular charcoal and lighter fluid (see page 154), or you can buy them ready-made (Matchlight). I like to bag my charcoal in zip-seal bags according to the amount I will need for a given recipe. Bagging it ahead of time means that

★ I will have enough but don't have to haul a lot extra.

★ I don't have to handle it as much at the cookout site.

★ I can hand each cooking group a bag of charcoal premeasured for their recipe.

For more information, see pages 149–157. For information on other fuel sources you can use with your Dutch oven, see pages 157–165 and 165–169.

6. EXTINGUISHING CAN

When my cookout is done, I use a new metal gallon-size paint can to extinguish my charcoal. This works great because when the charcoal is in the can and I put the lid on, the coals go out almost instantly and the can is cool enough to carry within twenty minutes.

One of the most important features of the extinguishing can is that it allows you to easily carry out what you carried in. Coals that have been extinguished in this manner can be reused (see page 155).

For information on purchasing an extinguishing can, see page 127. For another extinguishing option, see page 34.

7. A PLAN

To get started: (1) choose your recipe or recipes and measure out the ingredients; (2) bag and treat your charcoal or buy a fresh bag of treated charcoal and count out what you need for each recipe; (3) grab your water, extinguishing can, Dutch Oven Kit, and Dutch oven(s); and (4) don't forget your book—*Dutch Oven Cookout: Step-by-Step*.

Using the steps, you can cook out on a driveway, walkway, stone patio, or hard-packed dirt, and the area will be no worse for the wear when you are done.

From start to finish, your cookout will usually take 2–2½ hours. For hints on planning for a large group cookout, see Section 4: "Planning for Groups," page 180.

SECTION 1: *Getting Ready*

SECTION 2:
The Cookout Steps

IMPORTANT REMINDERS   22
STEP 1: SETUP   23
STEP 2: LIGHT   25
STEP 3: PREHEAT & SEASON   27
STEP 4: FRY/SIMMER   29

STEP 5: BAKE   31
STEP 6: EXTINGUISH & EAT   33
STEP 7: CLEAN   35
IN CASE OF RAIN   38

The steps are 1) Setup; 2) Light; 3) Preheat & Season; 4) Fry/Simmer; 5) Bake; 6) Extinguish & Eat; and 7) Clean.

IMPORTANT REMINDERS

★ Avoid dropping the Dutch oven, especially on hard surfaces. If the Dutch oven is too heavy, carry the lid separate from the bottom.

★ Use the Dutch Oven Kit equipment only for its intended purpose, such as using tongs only for moving coals, using the ash brush only for ashes.

★ Avoid using metal utensils or knives when cooking in your Dutch oven—they can scratch the nonstick seasoning coat.

★ Don't leave the coals burning on the lid longer than recommended. This can cause the seasoning coat on the lid to burn away. If this should happen, make sure to store the Dutch oven in a dry location and reseason the outside of the lid the next time you cook.

★ Be aware of food safety and personal safety—Keep your cold foods cold and hot foods hot. Keep raw meat away from ready-to-eat foods. Always use the hammer or gloves to lift the Dutch oven or extinguishing bucket. Keep first-aid supplies nearby.

★ Take out everything you take in—leave your cookout area as clean as or cleaner than you found it.

STEP 1: SETUP
Time: 10 minutes

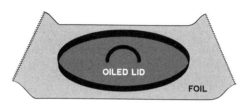

1. Select a cooking spot on rock, cement, or hard-packed ground away from plants or flammable materials.

2. Oil the Dutch oven and lid:

- Pour 1 teaspoon or more of vegetable oil into the Dutch oven.
- Gather the corners of the paper towel and twist them together. Hold on to this "handle" and use the puffy part of the towel to spread the oil.
- Start with the inside of the lid and pot, and then do the outside. Keep the towel to use later.

3. Put down a sheet of foil and place the oiled lid (oiled side down) in the center of it. Set the pot aside.

SECTION 2: *The Cookout Steps*

SETUP FAQS

Why oil the Dutch oven?

- It is the first step in seasoning. (See "Preheat & Season FAQs," page 28.)
- By oiling the Dutch oven during **Setup**, you avoid having to oil it when it is hot.

How much oil should I use?

- You should use as much oil as will stick to the oven without creating puddles. If your Dutch oven is relatively new, you may need a little more oil.

Why put down foil?

- Foil keeps the oiled lid clean and protects the ground a little bit from the hot coals.
- The foil will serve as a way to package up your ashes when you are done.

Why put the lid down before the pot?

- You will be using the lid as a place to light the coals.
- Lighting the coals on the lid helps protect the ground from the heat of the coals and starts to preheat the lid.

STEP 2: LIGHT
Time: 20-40 minutes

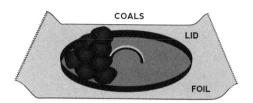

1. Pile "easy-light" coals on the lid in a tall pyramid shape as shown in the diagram. (You can support the coals against the rim and handle.) If using more than 16 coals, you should create multiple pyramids on the lid with 10–16 coals in each pile. (Charcoal amounts are given in the recipes and on page 150.)

2. Move anything flammable several feet away from the coals. Light the coals with a match by holding the match under the corner of one of the coals until the coal catches.

3. Leave the coals in a pile and allow them to burn for 20–40 minutes or until about 80 percent of each coal has turned gray.

4. While the coals light, read through the remaining cookout steps and your recipe.

LIGHT FAQS

Why do I stack the charcoal like a pyramid?

The higher and narrower the pyramid is, the faster the coals will light; however, if you have too many coals in your pyramid, the inside coals will not get enough oxygen. This is why you should have 10–16 coals in each pyramid.

How can I tell if the coals have started?

When you hold a match to the coals, the lighter fluid in the coals will start to burn with a flame. This flame will continue for a while and then go out.

How can I tell if the coals are still lighting after the flame goes out?

Hold your hand over the coals—they should be hot! Also, you can fan the coals and see them glow red.

Do I really have to wait until 80 percent of each coal has turned gray?

Charcoal doesn't reach its full heat until it is fully lit. If you spread out your coals before they are lit, it will take 2–3 times longer for your food to cook, or it may not cook at all.

Is there anything I can do to make it light faster?

Make sure your coals were recently treated and kept dry or purchased new. Make the pyramid as tall as you can. Turn the top coals over partway through and check the middle coals. If you are really in a hurry, you can use a pie tin or similar object to fan the coals—the extra air movement can help them light faster.

STEP 3: PREHEAT & SEASON

Time: 20 minutes

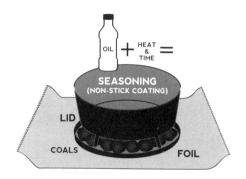

1. Once the coals are lit and are 80 percent gray, spread them out in a single layer on the lid.

2. Place the oiled pot over the coals, shifting the charcoal as needed to make room for the legs. As the pot heats, it will "season"—the oil will begin to bake on and form a hard, nonstick coating. If puddles of oil form in the pot as the pot heats, soak the extra oil up with a paper towel.

3. When the oil starts to smoke and the bottom of the pot starts to look dry instead of glossy, wipe the inside lightly once more with the oily paper towel and go on to the next step.

PREHEAT & SEASON FAQS

Why should I preheat?

- Preheating the oven sanitizes it— it kills any germs and releases any moisture or odors trapped in the oven. If you lean over the pot and sniff you will probably catch a whiff of whatever was last cooked in that Dutch oven. After a few minutes of seasoning this smell will go away and be replaced by a neutral "hot" smell.
- Preheating means that food will cook faster and more evenly—it will taste better and be safer.

Why should I season?

- Seasoning the inside protects the iron oven from the moisture in foods and seasoning the outside protects the iron from moisture in the environment.
- Seasoning creates a nonstick coating and makes the oven easier to clean.

What if I cut this step short?

- The oil needs heat to form the hard, nonstick coating called seasoning. If the seasoning doesn't harden or dry, you may have problems with food sticking or even rust. A well-seasoned Dutch oven should have a smooth, hard surface, and foods should come away easily from the sides, leaving the Dutch oven mostly clean when you serve up. See page 105.

STEP 4: FRY/SIMMER

Time: 15–20 min. for Fry; 20–60 min. for Simmer

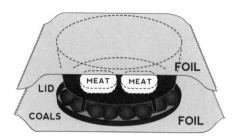

*Use **Fry/Simmer** to cook quickly at a higher temperature (sauté) or to simmer. See recipe for exact instructions. If your recipe does not require you to cook anything using **Fry/Simmer**, you can go directly to the next step.*

1. Place food to be fried (sautéed) or simmered in the pot and cover loosely with foil to help trap the steam. If the coals are fully lit and you have properly preheated and seasoned, the food will sizzle when you add it to the pot. You can curl the foil under the handles on either side of the Dutch oven to keep it from blowing away.

2. Stir or turn the food every 5 minutes or so while you are frying, every 10 minutes or so when simmering.

3. For casseroles and soups that have raw meat as an ingredient, you should cook the meat well before adding other ingredients. **Fry** frozen meat for 10–15 minutes, then break it into pieces and cook 5 more minutes or until meat looks and smells done. If desired, you can add dry seasonings to the meat during the final 5 minutes or so. This will help hydrate the spices and blend flavors.

SECTION 2: *The Cookout Steps*

FRY/SIMMER FAQS

My recipe tells me to take the pot off of the heat after I Preheat & Season, and then it says to put it back on the heat to Simmer—Why?

Allowing the pot to cool slightly after **Preheat & Season** can help prevent foods containing milk or sugar from burning when you first add them. Safety tip: When adding liquids to an empty preheated pot, hold your hand to the side instead of over the pot to avoid steam burns.

STEP 5: BAKE
Time: 15–30 minutes

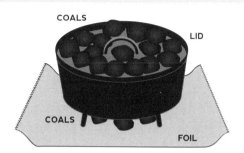

*Use **Bake** to cook foods that can burn easily or that you would bake in an oven at home (cobblers, casseroles, breads.) See recipe for exact instructions. If your recipe doesn't have a **Bake** step, go on to Step 6.*

1. Using a leather glove, move the pot to the side. Use the hammer or lid-lifter to lift the lid with the charcoal onto the pot.

2. Using tongs, place a quarter of the total number of coals in a circle on the foil. Using a glove, lift the pot with the lid back onto the foil. Center the Dutch oven over the coals. The circle of coals should be just smaller than the bottom of the pot.

3. Spread the remaining coals across the lid, with more around the edges than in the center. While the food bakes, you can clean up your area and get ready to eat.

4. Check for doneness before going on to the next step.

BAKE FAQS

How do I know if the food is done?

- With most recipes, you should wait to check it until you can smell it. When the recipe is close to done, you should be able to smell it, even though the lid is still on.

- Recipes with cheese on top: if the cheese is melted, the food is probably done, and you can do a taste test.

- Recipes with biscuits or cake on top: touch the biscuit or cake mix lightly in the middle. If it is still sticky or collapses when you touch it, it is not done. When the batter or dough is cooked, it should spring back when touched.

Will my food burn if I bake it too long?

- With the coals arranged as described above, it is almost impossible for the food to burn while it is baking. Especially with cobblers, an extra 5–10 minutes usually won't hurt and will help it not to be doughy. The exception to this is if your food rises up enough to touch the inside of the lid—then it is possible for the very top to burn.

Is there anything special I need to do during Bake if the weather is windy or cold?

- If you are cooking in windy conditions, you may need to weight down the corners of the foil under the Dutch oven during **Bake**.

- If you are cooking in very cold or windy weather the coals will burn out faster and you will need to add more coals partway through. See page 154 for details.

STEP 6: EXTINGUISH & EAT

Time: 25-40 minutes

Coals go out when they have no oxygen.

1. After you have finished ***Frying/Simmering*** or ***Baking***—before you eat—you should extinguish the charcoal. Use tongs to move the lumps of charcoal to the bucket, and then set the lid on top. The coals will go out almost immediately. Do not touch the can—it will be hot!

2. Use the hammer to lift, turn and tip the lid of the Dutch oven so you can dump the ashes off onto the foil. You can lightly tap the lid against the foil while holding it with the hammer to get most of the ashes off. Put the lid back on the pot and use an ash brush to dust remaining ashes off the lid. Bring the sides of the foil together and fold down the top and ends around the ashes like you are wrapping a sandwich. Allow the packet of ashes to cool completely before disposing of it. (See also FAQ on page 179.)

3. Remember to use gloves when handling the extinguishing bucket for the first 10 to 15 minutes after you put the coals in. Do not place the bucket near flammable materials until it is completely cool to the touch.

EXTINGUISH FAQS

Why should we extinguish before we eat?

- It will take time for the charcoal bucket to cool down; by extinguishing before you eat, you allow more cooling time.

- If the coals are left on or under the Dutch oven while you serve and eat, the food is more likely to burn on, and the pot will be harder to clean. Also, you will be more likely to get ash in the food while you are serving it. (Eating a little ash won't hurt you; it just isn't very appetizing!)

- Most of the recipes taste better if they sit covered for 10–15 minutes after they finish cooking. The Dutch oven will keep the food hot, so you can wait until all the food is done and serve it as a buffet.

Will the coals really go out if I just set the lid on?

Yes, as long as the lid isn't warped. If you want to make doubly sure the coals will go out, put on gloves and gently seal the lid. Avoid the temptation to pound the lid onto the extinguishing bucket—this will make it difficult to remove next time and isn't really necessary

What should I do if I don't have an extinguishing bucket?

If you don't have an extinguishing bucket, you can also extinguish by submerging each coal (one at a time) in a can of water (a fruit or soup can from one of the recipes works well.) Submerge for about 10 seconds, and then remove. Make sure they are cold to the touch before disposing of them.

STEP 7: CLEAN
Time: 5–10 minutes

1. As soon as you are done serving, transfer any remaining food to another container. Scrape the pot thoroughly with the plastic pot scraper. When you are done, it should look mostly clean. Don't forget to scrape the serving spoons.

2. Add 1–2 inches of water and a squirt or two of biodegradable soap to the pot. Scrub the pot with a soft fir or spruce cone, giving special attention to the sides where food may have baked on. You can also soak and scrub the serving spoons and pot scraper. Use the damp fir cone to scrub the inside of the lid.

3. Pour the water out of the pot (go away from the cookout site to do this.) Dry the pot and lid with a paper towel. If any spots still look dirty, scrub and dry them again.

4. Store the pot with a clean paper towel inside it to absorb any remaining moisture.

5. Don't forget to put all equipment away and leave your cookout area clean!

CLEAN FAQS

Why is it important to scrape?

- Scraping thoroughly will make the rest of the job easier.
- Removing as much food as possible before step two means that fewer food particles will end up in the environment, keeping the cookout area nicer and the animals healthier.

I thought soap and/or water could hurt the Dutch oven seasoning?

- As long as you have let the oil bake on during **Preheat & Season**, it cannot be removed with mild soap and water. Oil that has not baked on may be removed, but this is good because unseasoned oil can cause your Dutch oven to become sticky.
- If there are areas on your Dutch oven that do not have a thick baked-on seasoning coat, water could make rust appear in those areas. Prevent this by seasoning well, cleaning the Dutch oven when it is warm, and drying it thoroughly after cleaning.

Why use a spruce/fir cone to clean with?

- It is renewable, disposable, and biodegradable. You can throw it away when you are done, which means you don't have to put something wet in your Dutch Oven Kit.
- It works better for this than most other scrubbers, and it won't melt with heat or scratch the seasoning coat.

What is the best time to clean the Dutch oven?

It is easier to clean the Dutch oven while it is still warm. If the pot is still warm, it will help heat up the water you pour into it. If the pot has cooled off, you may be washing with cold water. This isn't as pleasant, but it's not a big deal as long as the pot ends up looking clean with no baked-on areas. The pot will be sanitized during **Preheat & Season** when you next use it.

Any suggestions for cleaning other dishes?

After food scraps have been scraped into the garbage, you can clean plates and utensils by scrubbing them with a handful of dry pine needles from the forest floor. If the food residue hasn't dried on, this method can be surprisingly effective. Dry pine needles are practically germ-free and make a great degreaser. Finish the process by rinsing the dishes or utensils with hot water.

There have been bear sightings in my area—do I need to take extra precautions when cleaning my Dutch oven?

If you are in an area with bears, even the small amounts of food that are left in the wash water could attract bears. In those situations, use a very small amount of water during **Clean** and pour all your wash water into a bucket. Take the bucket far from camp to dump it or, if you have access to a toilet, dump it there. Take care to clean up even small particles that fall on the ground. Consult with a forest service expert if you are unsure what to do.

IN CASE OF RAIN

PREPARE AHEAD—Prepare for rain by bringing string and tarps, and rain ponchos or rain jackets to your cookout. If cooking out at home, set up a collapsible awning or use a porch or carport area for your cookout. Charcoal may be harder to light in damp weather, so bring extra lighter fluid and make sure you have plenty of matches—matches can also be much harder to light when there is water vapor in the air. Make sure the charcoal stays completely dry until it is time to light it.

PROTECT THE COALS—While the coals are still flaming (during *Step 2: Light*), a light rain will not hurt them. After the flames go out and while cooking during *Step 5: Bake*, you can make a tent out of foil to protect the coals (see photo), or build a shelter over the whole area with a tarp. Keep the rain off the coals as much as possible as you *Preheat & Season* and *Fry/Simmer* and especially as you *Bake*.

PROTECT THE EQUIPMENT—Hammers, can openers, extinguishing buckets, and other equipment can rust or be ruined by water. Get them out of the rain and dry them off as soon as you can. If your Dutch Oven Kit becomes damp inside, open it up later to dry.

PROTECT YOURSELF—If there is no danger of lightning, a tree can keep you mostly dry for ten minutes of heavy rain. Put on a jacket or poncho.

SECTION 3:
The Recipes

HOW TO USE THE RECIPES   40

PLANNING YOUR MENU   42

STANDARD INGREDIENT LIST 44

SUPER-EASY RECIPES 49

EASY RECIPES   61

INTERMEDIATE RECIPES 73

Dutch Oven Buffet left to right: Eight-inch Dutch ovens with Cowboy Potatoes, Chicken &
Broccoli, Shepherd's Pie, Taco Soup

HOW TO USE THE RECIPES

USING THE STEPS WITH THE RECIPES: Large bold text in the recipe refers the cook back to the cookout steps pages (such as ***Preheat & Season***, ***Fry/Simmer***, ***Bake***)

STANDARD INGREDIENT LIST: All recipe ingredients are listed in the Standard Ingredient List. Detailed information about each ingredient is given in the list. Most of the ingredients are used in several recipes and always in the same amounts. For example, sour cream appears in many recipes, and the 1x recipe always calls for eight ounces. A few recipes use two times the Standard Ingredient List amount and this is noted in the recipe.

LIQUIDS: Juice or water in canned goods is intended to be part of the recipe unless otherwise indicated in the recipe. If water is called for as part of a recipe, the amount is usually given in terms of one of the cans used in the recipe as well as in cups or ounces. For example, a recipe might call for "½ soup can of water." This is so you can use what you already have on hand—the can you just emptied—to do your measuring. Just don't forget to keep your cans until you are done measuring!

ZIP-SEAL BAGS: If a recipe calls for a zip-seal bag, the bag is used for mixing ingredients. As an example, in Hot Fudge Cake, you would place the cake mix and the evaporated milk in the bag, seal it, squish the ingredients until well mixed, cut off a corner of the bag and dispense the contents into the Dutch oven as instructed in the recipe.

SCALING THE RECIPES: Each recipe has a table scaling the recipe for different Dutch oven sizes. The base (1x) recipe is the eight-inch or two-quart recipe. Recipe amounts for other Dutch oven sizes are multiplied from the base recipe. More information on scaling the recipes can be found in "Converting a Regular Recipe to a Dutch Oven Recipe," page 138.

CAN SIZES: In larger versions of the recipes, the can sizes given in the chart are just recommended sizes. You can add up the number of ounces you need of a given ingredient and select can sizes accordingly. Relative amounts are often changed in the chart for the ten-inch recipe to help avoid having to use "half a can" of a certain ingredient, so the ten-inch recipe will sometimes turn out a little different than all the other sizes. In recipes that use evaporated milk and water in the same step, the water/milk proportion is often changed to make the best use of the evaporated milk can sizes commercially available.

CHARCOAL AMOUNTS: When making a shopping list for multiple recipes, I add up the total amount of charcoal I will need, then divide that number by 16. The result is the number of pounds of charcoal you will need. This works because there are usually just over 16 coals in a pound of charcoal.

ALTITUDE: Altitude adjustments are generally not necessary for these recipes. The recipes were all tested extensively and successfully at altitudes of 4000 and 8000 feet.

TIME: When making the recipes in this book, you should allow 2–2½ hours for your cookout, including eating and cleanup.

PLANNING YOUR MENU

Here are some sample menu plans and menu planning ideas to help you get started.

....

Easy Favorites for 3 to 5:

APPETIZER: baby carrots or optional .5x Cornbread

MAIN COURSE: 1x Cheesy Chicken

DESSERT: 1x Peach Cobbler

This menu requires two eight-inch Dutch ovens and an optional ten-inch if doing the Cornbread. Cheesy Chicken is super popular with all ages and quick-cooking. Peach Cobbler is a classic Dutch oven recipe anyway, and the Peach Cobbler recipe in this book is the best I've had . . . if I do say so myself! Without the Cornbread, this menu requires about two pounds of charcoal.

....

South of the Border Night for 6 to 8:

APPETIZER: 1x Nacho Cheese Sauce (eight-inch Dutch oven), served with tortilla chips and salsa

MAIN COURSE: 2x Chicken Spanish Rice (twelve-inch Dutch oven), served with salad

DESSERT: 1x Kara's Razzmatazz (eight-inch Dutch oven)

This menu requires two eight-inch Dutch ovens and one twelve-inch. In shopping for this menu, I would buy a big bag of tortilla chips, take out the amount I needed for the Chicken Spanish Rice, then use the rest for the appetizer. This menu requires about four pounds of charcoal.

Dutch Oven Buffet for 10 to 15:

APPETIZER: Veggie Tray

MAIN COURSE: 1x Cheesy Chicken, 1x Cowboy Potatoes, 1x Chicken Enchiladas, 1x Lasagna, 1x Taco Soup

DESSERT: 3x Hot Fudge Cake

This menu requires five eight-inch Dutch Ovens and one fourteen-inch Dutch oven. It requires about eight pounds of charcoal. This is a good menu for youth groups or other groups that want to have a hands-on cooking experience (or need to!). The menu offers several options and makes it easy to accommodate different diet needs or picky eaters. When doing this kind of menu, it works well to wait until everything is done and then set it up as buffet. If you want to serve the buffet on a table, cover the table with old towels and set the hot Dutch ovens on the towels.

COMMON MEASUREMENT CONVERSIONS:
1 cup = 8 ounces = ½ pint

4 Tablespoons = ¼ cup

3 teaspoons = 1 Tablespoon

1 cube butter = ½ cup = 4 ounces = 8 Tablespoons

STANDARD INGREDIENT LIST

Amounts given in this list are the amounts needed for the 1x recipe (unless otherwise indicated).

Refrigerated and Frozen

- **GROUND BEEF** = two frozen hamburger patties or ½ lb. super extra lean ground beef. Can be divided and frozen ahead of time.
- **CHICKEN** = 4–6 frozen chicken tenders or 8–12 ounces of boneless, skinless chicken breast. Can be frozen ahead of time. Tip: If using chicken breast, buy it fresh and cut it into slices before you freeze it—this will make it faster and easier to cook.
- **BACON** = 8 slices of precooked bacon, torn or cut into pieces. Precooked bacon can be kept in a cool, non-refrigerated place for several days. An easy way to cut precooked bacon into pieces is with scissors or kitchen shears.
- **EGGS** = 1 cup liquid egg product or 4 whole medium eggs. Liquid egg product is easy to transport and can be frozen. If frozen, it can take several days in an ice chest to thaw.
- **CHEESE** = 1½ cups (5–6 oz.) shredded cheddar or mozzarella as specified. Can be frozen ahead of time.
- **SOUR CREAM** = 1 cup (8 ounces)
- **COTTAGE CHEESE/RICOTTA CHEESE** = 1 to 1½ cups or 8–12 oz.
- **BUTTER** = ⅓ of a cube (2–3 Tbsp., 1.3 oz.). Can be frozen ahead of time.
- **REFRIGERATED CHEESE TORTELLINI** = 9-oz. or about 40 count
- **REFRIGERATOR BISCUITS** = 16-oz. can jumbo buttermilk

biscuits (recipe may call for $\frac{1}{2}$ can or 8-oz. can)

- **FLOUR TORTILLAS** = Can use either precooked or ready-to-cook. Eight-inch or ten-inch tortillas recommended, depending on the size of Dutch oven you are using. (For more info, see Fajitas, page 76.)
- **FROZEN DINNER ROLLS** = 10 frozen balls of dough, each roll approximately $1\frac{1}{3}$ to 2 oz.
- **POTATOES** = 1 lb. (approx. $3\frac{1}{2}$ cups) frozen cubed potatoes
- **FROZEN VEGETABLE** = 1 to $1\frac{1}{2}$ cups (petite peas, corn, chopped spinach, chopped broccoli—see recipe)

Produce

- **APPLE** = 4–5 medium apples
- **PEPPER** = half of a red or yellow bell pepper
- **ONION** = half of a large yellow onion
- **TOMATO** = 1 whole Roma or other medium tomato
- **FRESH SLICED OR CUBED VEGETABLE** = $1–1\frac{1}{2}$ cups (carrots, zucchini)

Canned

- **SOUP** = 10-oz. can condensed soup, various types as specified (for larger recipes, 28-oz. "family size" can)
- **BROTH** = 14-or 15-oz. can. Different types depending on the recipe.
- **PETITE DICED TOMATOES** = 15-oz. can (for larger recipes, 28-oz. can). Petite diced works better than regular diced canned tomatoes.
- **TOMATO SAUCE** = 8-oz. can
- **CORN** = 8-oz can (for larger recipes, 16-oz. can)

- **GREEN BEANS** = 8-oz. can (for larger recipes, 16-oz. can). Can also use "no-added-salt" green beans.
- **CHINESE VEGETABLES** = 16-oz. can
- **SLICED MUSHROOMS** = 6-oz. can
- **GREEN CHILES** = diced, 4-oz. can
- **WESTERN-STYLE CHILI BEANS** = 15-oz. can
- **OLIVES** = sliced, 2.2-oz. can (for larger recipes, 3.8-oz. can)
- **EVAPORATED MILK** = 5-oz. can (for larger recipes, 12-oz. can)
- **CRUSHED PINEAPPLE** = 8-oz. can
- **CANNED FRUIT** = 16-oz. can. Fruit canned in light syrup or fruit juice preferred.
- **PIE FILLINGS** = 20-oz. can (recipe may call for half can)
- **FROSTING** = 16-oz. can (recipe may call for half can)

Dry

- **INSTANT RICE** = 1½ cups. Instead of 1½ cups instant rice, you can use 1 cup converted or short grain; however, your recipe will take 10–15 minutes longer to cook, and, depending on the recipe and weather, you may need to light another batch of charcoal. See page 153 for more information.
- **RICE-A-RONI** = 1 (7-oz.) package "Parmesan chicken" or other flavor
- **INSTANT MASHED POTATO FLAKES** = 1½ cups potato *flakes* (If using potato powder, use ¼ cup plus 1 Tbsp. with the same amount of water. Do not use potato pearls with this recipe.)
- **CURLY EGG NOODLES** = quarter pound or about 2½ cups medium noodles, uncooked
- **TORTILLA CHIPS** = 2 ounces or about 14 large triangle chips

(enough to make two layers in an empty 2-quart Dutch oven or enough to loosely fill a quart zip-seal bag.)

- **FRITOS** = ½ pound (~1 quart)
- **CRACKERS** (low fat recommended) = 10 round (Ritz-style) crackers = about 32 grams
- **CORNBREAD/MUFFIN MIXES** = 7–8-oz. mixes (about 1½ cups mix). Jiffy brand works well.
- **CAKE MIXES** = half of a 16–18-oz. package (just under 2 cups)
- **PUDDING MIXES** = 3.5-oz. box **cook & serve** pudding (not instant)
- **FLOUR** = ¼ cup (4 Tbsp.) all-purpose flour

Seasonings

- **GARLIC SALT** = as called for. Usually ½ tsp. for eight-inch recipe.
- **CINNAMON SUGAR MIX** = ¾ cup sugar mixed with 1 tsp. cinnamon
- **ONION** = 1 Tbsp. dry minced onion or half of a whole, fresh onion, diced. If using fresh onion, sauté it 5–10 minutes during *Fry/Simmer* before adding the next ingredients.
- **BASIL** = 1 Tbsp. dry leaf basil
- **PARMESAN CHEESE** = 3 Tbsp. grated Parmesan or similar cheese
- **SEASONING OR SAUCE MIXES** = 1–2-oz. grocery store packet or 2–3 Tbsp. various seasoning mixes as specified in recipe: enchilada seasoning, fajita seasoning, fried rice seasoning (Kikkoman brand recommended), ranch dressing mix, taco seasoning, spaghetti seasoning, stir-fry seasoning (get the kind that says, "just add water")

SUPER-EASY RECIPES

MAIN AND SIDE DISHES

Cheesy Chicken   50
Chicken and Broccoli   51
Corn Chowder   52
Cowboy Potatoes   53

Hearty Breakfast   54
Nacho Cheese Sauce   55
Taco Soup   56
Tomato Basil Soup   58

BREADS AND DESSERTS

Cornbread   59

Fourth of July Cake   60

SECTION 3: The Recipes

CHEESY CHICKEN

1. *Preheat & Season. Fry* chicken. Sprinkle with garlic salt if desired.

2. Add cream of chicken soup, water, sour cream, cheese, and rice. Stir.

3. *Bake* 10–20 minutes or until rice is soft.

INGREDIENT	8" (1x)	10" (1.5x)	12" (2x)	14" (3x)
chicken tenders	4–6 (½ lb.)	6–9 (¾ lb.)	8–12 (1 lb.)	12–18 (1½ lbs.)
cream of chicken soup	10-oz. can	1½ (10-oz.) cans	2 (10-oz.) cans	28-oz. can or 3 (10-oz.) cans
sour cream	8 oz. (1 cup)	12 oz. (1½ cups)	16 oz. (2 cups)	24 oz. (3 cups)
shredded cheddar	~6 oz. (~1½ cups)	~9 oz. (~2¼ cups)	~12 oz. (~3 cups)	~1 lb. (~4½ cups)
instant rice	1½ cups	$2^1/_4$ cups	3 cups	4½ cups
water	½ (10-oz.) soup can (½ cup + 2 Tbsp.)	¾ (10-oz.) soup can (1 cup)	1 soup can (10 oz.)	½ (28-oz.) soup can (15 oz. or 2 cups)
SERVES	4–5	6–8	8–10	12–16
CHARCOAL	16	25	36	49

★ This recipe uses "same-depth" conversions. It can also be done using "maximum volume conversions" (see page 140). Bake time will be longer for maximum volume recipes in larger Dutch ovens.

★ This is an easy popular recipe—a good one to try first.

★ MEAT-FREE: leave out the chicken; use cream of celery soup.

★ GLUTEN-FREE: use gluten-free cream of chicken or cream of celery soup. Make sure you also use gluten-free rice.

CHICKEN AND BROCCOLI

1. *Preheat & Season*. *Fry* chicken. Sprinkle with garlic salt if desired.

2. Add mushrooms, broccoli, sour cream, Rice-a-Roni, and seasoning packet from rice. Add water. Stir.

3. *Bake* 45–55 minutes or until rice is soft. If too dry, stir in a little water.

INGREDIENT	8" (1x)	10" (1.5x)	12" (2x)	14" (3x)
chicken tenders	4–6 (½ lb.)	6–9 (¾ lb.)	8–12 (1 lb.)	12–18 (1½ lb.)
sliced mushrooms (with liquid)	6-oz. can	1½ or 2 (6-oz.) cans	2 (6-oz.) cans	3 (6-oz.) cans
broccoli cuts	1–1½ cups	1½ –2 cups	2–3 cups	3–5 cups
sour cream	8 oz. (1 cup)	12 oz. (1½ cups)	16 oz. (2 cups)	24 oz. (3 cups)
Parmesan Chicken Rice-a-Roni	1 pkg.	1½ pkgs.	2 pkgs.	3 pkgs.
water	$1\frac{1}{3}$ mushroom cans (~1 cup)	2 mushroom cans (~1½ cups)	$2\frac{2}{3}$ mushroom cans (~2 cups)	4 mushroom cans (~3 cups)
SERVES	4–5	6–8	8–10	12–16
CHARCOAL	18	28	39	53

★ This is one of my favorite recipes, but it does *Bake* longer than several other recipes in the book. If you plan to use it as part of a Dutch oven buffet, you may want to start it about 15 minutes before other recipes.

★ Can leave out mushrooms and add an additional ¾ cup water per 1x recipe.

★ MEAT-FREE: leave out the chicken, and use a different flavor of Rice-a-Roni.

SECTION 3: The Recipes

CORN CHOWDER

1. After you **Preheat & Season**, break or cut bacon into small pieces and add to Dutch oven. **Fry** 3–5 minutes. Add potatoes and **Fry** 10 minutes.

2. Add soup, corn, cheese, milk, water, and a few shakes of pepper. Stir.

3. Cover with foil. **Simmer** 15–20 minutes.

INGREDIENT	8" (1x)	10" (1.5x)	12" (2x)	14" (3x)
bacon (precooked)	8 slices	12 slices	16 slices	24 slices
potatoes	1 lb.	1½ lbs.	2 lbs.	3 lbs.
cream of mushroom soup	10-oz. can	1½ (10-oz.) cans	2 (10-oz.) cans	28-oz. can
corn	8-oz. can	16 oz. can	16 oz. can	16-oz. + 8-oz. can
shredded cheddar	6 oz. (1½ cups)	9 oz. (2¼ cups)	12 oz. (3 cups)	18 oz. (4½ cups)
evaporated milk	5-oz. can	5-oz. can	12-oz. can	12-oz. can
water	1 milk can (½ cup + 2 Tbsp.)	1½ milk cans or 1 cup	⅔ milk can* or 1 cup	1⅓ milk cans* or 2 cups
SERVES	4–5	6–8	8–10	12–16
CHARCOAL	16	25	36	49

*Please note water amounts for twelve-inch and fourteen-inch are based on the use of a 12-oz. can of evaporated milk.

★ This recipe uses "same-depth" conversions. It can also be done using "maximum volume conversions" (see page 140). Simmer time will be longer for maximum volume recipes in larger Dutch ovens.

★ MEAT-FREE: leave out bacon and add dry onion if desired.

★ GLUTEN-FREE: use gluten-free soup and gluten-free bacon.

★ Good served with Cornbread or Parmesan Pull-aparts.

COWBOY POTATOES

1. After you *Preheat & Season*, break or cut bacon into small pieces and add to Dutch oven. Add butter and onion. Stir. Allow butter to melt.

2. Add potatoes and water (water measurement doesn't have to be exact). Cover with foil. *Fry* 15 minutes, stirring twice.

3. Sprinkle with salt & pepper, as desired. Add the peas and half the cheese. Stir. Sprinkle top with rest of cheese.

4. *Bake* 10–15 minutes.

INGREDIENT	8" (1x)	10" (2x)	12" (3x)	14" (4x)
bacon (precooked)	8 slices	16 slices	24 slices	32 slices
onion (dry)	1 Tbsp.	2 Tbsp.	3 Tbsp.	1/4 cup
butter	$^1/_3$ cube	$^2/_3$ cube	1 cube	$1^1/_3$ cube
potatoes (frozen, cubed)	1 lb.	2 lb.	3 lb.	4 lb.
peas (frozen)	1 cup	2 cups	3 cups	4 cups
shredded cheddar	6 oz. (~1½ cups)	12 oz. (~3 cups)	18 oz. (~4½ cups)	24 oz. (~6 cups)
water	½ to $^3/_4$ cup	~1½ cups	~$2^1/_4$ cups	~3 cups
SERVES	3–5	6–10	9–15	12–20
CHARCOAL	16	25	36	49

★ The recipe conversions here are "maximum volume" conversions (see page 141). Cook times may be slightly longer for larger Dutch ovens.

★ MEAT-FREE: leave out bacon.

★ GLUTEN-FREE: use gluten-free bacon.

HEARTY BREAKFAST

1. After you **Preheat & Season**, break or cut bacon into small pieces and add to Dutch oven. **Fry** 5 minutes. Add potatoes. Cover with foil. **Fry** 15 minutes, stirring 2–3 times.

2. Add eggs, about $1/8$ tsp. salt, a dash of pepper, and half the cheese. Stir until all ingredients are mixed and egg starts to cook. Sprinkle top with rest of cheese.

3. *Bake* 10–20 minutes.

INGREDIENT	8" (1x)	10" (1.5x)	12" (2x)	14" (3x)
bacon (precooked)	8 slices	12 slices	16 slices	24 slices
potatoes	1 lb.	1½ lbs.	2 lbs.	3 lbs.
egg product (eggs) (2x standard amount)	2 cups (8 eggs)	3 cups (1 dozen)	4 cups (16 eggs)	6 cups (2 dozen)
shredded cheddar	6 oz. (~1½ cups)	9 oz. (~2¼ cups)	12 oz. (~3 cups)	18 oz. (~4½ cups)
SERVES	4–6	6–9	8–12	12–18
CHARCOAL	16	25	36	49

★ If your Dutch oven is well seasoned and well preheated, the egg will come easily away from the sides as you stir in step 2 and as you serve it. Make sure to remove from heat as soon as it is done cooking.

★ Good with ketchup or salsa.

★ Can use sausage instead of bacon.

★ MEAT-FREE: leave out bacon and add onion if desired.

★ GLUTEN-FREE: use gluten-free bacon.

NACHO CHEESE SAUCE

1. After you **Preheat & Season**, pour milk and green chiles into the Dutch oven.

2. Add half the cheese. Stir. **Simmer** until cheese starts to melt. Stir in remaining cheese. **Simmer** while stirring until sauce is smooth.

3. Reduce heat (take away about half the coals from under the Dutch oven). Keep warm, stirring occasionally. Serve with tortilla chips.

INGREDIENT	8" (1x)*	10" (2x)*	12" (3x)*
evaporated milk	5-oz. can	12-oz. can	12-oz. can + 5-oz. can
green chiles	4-oz. can	2 (4-oz.) cans	3 (4-oz.) cans
shredded cheddar (2x standard amount)	12 oz. (~3 cups)	24 oz. (~6 cups)	36 oz. (~9 cups)
SERVES	6–8	12–16	18–24
CHARCOAL	16	25	36

*2x batch can also be done in an eight-inch and 3x can be done in a ten-inch.

★ For milder flavor use ½ can of green chiles for the 1x recipe and 1 can for the 2x.

★ Fast and easy (only takes about 10 minutes after **Preheat & Season**). You can do this as an appetizer then use the coals for something else.

★ Eat while warm!

SECTION 3: *The Recipes*

TACO SOUP

1. *Preheat & Season*. *Fry* meat. Add taco seasoning.
2. Open all cans. Drain the olives (only the olives!).
3. Add canned goods to meat in the order listed. Stir. Add water.
4. *Simmer* 20 minutes or longer.
5. Serve over corn chips, top with shredded cheddar and sour cream.*

INGREDIENT	8" (1x)	10" (1x)	12" (2x)	14" (3x)
ground beef	½ lb.		1 lb.	1½ lbs.
taco seasoning	2–3 Tbsp. (~1 pkt.)		4–6 Tbsp. (~2 pkts.)	6–9 Tbsp. (~ 3 pkts.)
petite diced tomatoes	15 oz.		28 oz.	15 oz. + 28 oz.
corn	8 oz.	Use 8" recipe	16 oz.	8 oz. + 16 oz.
chili beans	15 oz.		28 oz.	15 oz. + 28 oz.
sliced olives	2.2 oz.		3.8 oz.	3.8 oz.
water	½ (8-oz.) corn can or ½ cup		½ (16-oz.) corn can or 1 cup	¾ (16-oz.) corn can or 1½ cups
SERVES	5–7	5–7	10–14	15–21
CHARCOAL	16	25	36	49

*For the 1x recipe you will need as a topping about ½ lb. corn chips or tortilla chips, 5–6 ounces shredded cheddar and 8–16 ounces sour cream. I usually just include the Standard Ingredient List amounts of cheese and sour cream multiplied for whatever batch size I am doing.

★ This soup cooks well with *Simmer*, and can be done over a butane burner or on the stove. It tastes better the longer it simmers—up to 1 hour.

★ This recipe uses "same-depth" conversions. It can also be done using "maximum volume conversions" (see page 140). Simmer time will be longer for maximum volume recipes in larger Dutch ovens.

★ Make sure pot is well seasoned to avoid ending up with a metallic taste in the soup.

★ Taco Soup works well for a group—especially when you don't know how many people will be coming.

★ MEAT-FREE: Leave out the ground beef. Add ½ cup instant rice (for 1x recipe).

★ GLUTEN-FREE: use gluten-free taco seasoning and use drained and rinsed gluten-free pinto beans.

SECTION 3: *The Recipes*

TOMATO BASIL SOUP

1. *Preheat & Season.* Add tomatoes, tomato soup, milk, basil, and water. Stir.

2. *Simmer* 20 minutes. Stir in Parmesan cheese.

INGREDIENT	8" (1x)	10" (2x)	12" (3x)	14" (4x)
petite diced tomatoes	15-oz. can	28-oz.	28-oz. can + 15-oz. can	2 (28-oz.) cans
cream of tomato soup	10-oz. can	2 (10 oz.) cans	28-oz. can	28 oz. + 10 oz.
evaporated milk	5-oz. can	12-oz. can	12-oz. can + 5-oz. can	2 (12-oz.) cans
dried basil	1 Tbsp.	2 Tbsp.	3 Tbsp.	1/4 cup
Parmesan	3 Tbsp.	6 Tbsp.	1/2 cup	3/4 cup
water	1 milk can or 1/2 cup + 2 Tbsp.	2/3 (12-oz.) milk can or 1 cup	12-oz. milk can or 1 1/2 cups	1 1/3 (12-oz.) milk cans or 2 cups
SERVES	3–4	6–8	9–12	12–16
CHARCOAL	16	25	36	49

★ Serve with Parmesan Pull-aparts or Cornbread.

★ Make this in your kitchen on a cold winter day— it is super easy and yummy.

★ The recipe conversions here are "maximum volume" conversions (see page 141). Cook times may be slightly longer for larger Dutch ovens.

★ GLUTEN-FREE: use gluten-free cream of tomato soup.

CORNBREAD

1. *Preheat & Season.* Melt butter.

2. Add milk, water, and corn muffin mix. Stir just until mixed.

3. *Bake* 20–30 minutes.

INGREDIENT	8" (.5x)	8" (1x)	10" (1.5x)	12" (2x)	14" (3x)
butter	$^1/_3$ cube	$^2/_3$ cube	1 cube	$1^1/_3$ cubes	2 cubes
evaporated milk	5-oz. can	5-oz. can	12-oz. can	12-oz. can	2 (12-oz.) cans
water	none	1 milk can or $^1/_2$ cup +2 Tbsp.	$^1/_4$ milk can or 3 oz.	$^2/_3$ milk can or 1 cup	$^1/_2$ milk can or 6 oz.
7-oz. corn muffin mix	1 pkg.	2 pkgs.	3 pkgs.	4 pkgs.	6 pkgs.
SERVES	3–4	6–8	9–12	12–16	18–24
CHARCOAL	*	16	25	36	49

*Note that the .5x recipe is the base recipe here and uses the amounts from the Standard Ingredient List. The .5 recipe can be done in an eight-inch with 16 charcoal (it will be a little thinner and get done faster) or in a pie-tin inside your ten-inch with 25 charcoal.

★ GLUTEN-FREE: use equal amount gluten-free cornbread mix instead of regular mix.

SECTION 3: *The Recipes*

FOURTH OF JULY CAKE

1. *Preheat & Season.* Remove pot from heat. Place sour cream and water (half of the amount of sour cream) in pot.

2. Stir in muffin mixes. Stir until just combined—don't overmix. Sprinkle top with cinnamon sugar if desired.

3. *Bake* about 30 minutes or until browned on top and no longer gooey in the middle.

INGREDIENT	8" (1x)	10" (1.5x)	12" (2x)	14" (3x)
sour cream	8 oz. (1 cup)	12 oz. (1½ cups)	16 oz. (2 cups)	24 oz. (3 cups)
7-oz. raspberry muffin mix	1 box	2 boxes	2 boxes	3 boxes
7-oz. blueberry muffin mix	1 box	1 box	2 boxes	3 boxes
water*	½ cup or 4 oz.	¾ cup or 6 oz.	1 cup or 8 oz.	1½ cups or 12 oz.
SERVES	5–6	7–9	10–12	15–18
CHARCOAL	16	25	36	49

* You can use your sour cream container to measure your water— you will need half as much water as the sour cream you used.

★ Goes well with Hearty Breakfast.

★ This is a pretty breakfast cake—red, white, and blue.

★ You can make this the night before—it tastes even better the second day.

EASY RECIPES

MAIN AND SIDE DISHES

Chicken Enchiladas	62	Hamburger Soup	65
Chicken Spanish Rice	63	Oriental Fried Rice	66
Enchiladas	64	Shepherd's Pie	67

BREADS AND DESSERTS

Kara's Razzmatazz	68	Peach Cobbler	70
Parmesan Pull-aparts	69	Sticky Buns	72

SECTION 3: *The Recipes*

CHICKEN ENCHILADAS

1. *Preheat & Season*. *Fry* chicken.
2. Add soup, milk, water if called for, the green chiles, and half of the cheese. Stir.
3. Add tortilla chips and push them down into the mixture until they are covered. Sprinkle with the remaining cheese.
4. *Bake* 10–20 minutes.

INGREDIENT	8" (1x)	10" (1.5x)	12" (2x)	14" (3x)
chicken tenders	4–6 (½ lb.)	6–9 (³/₄ lb.)	8–12 (1 lb.)	12–18 (1½ lb.)
cream of chicken soup	10-oz. can	1½ (10-oz.) cans	2 (10-oz.) cans	28-oz. can or 3 (10-oz.) cans
evaporated milk	5-oz. can	5-oz. can	2 (5-oz. cans)	12-oz. can
water	none	½ milk can or 5 Tbsp.	none	¼ milk can or 3 oz.
shredded cheddar	6 oz. (1½ cups)	9 oz. (2¼ cups)	12 oz. (3 cups)	18 oz. (4½ cups)
green chiles	½ of (4-oz.) can	4-oz. can	4-oz. can	2 (4-oz.) cans
tortilla chips	2 oz.	3 oz.	4 oz.	6 oz.
SERVES	4–5	6–7	8–10	12–15
CHARCOAL	16	25	36	49

★ Tortilla chips should be 2 to 2½ chips deep.
★ GLUTEN-FREE: use gluten-free cream of chicken soup and gluten-free tortilla chips.

DUTCH OVEN COOKOUT, STEP BY STEP

CHICKEN SPANISH RICE

1. *Preheat & Season*. *Fry* meat. Add enchilada seasoning, tomatoes, and corn. Stir.

2. Sprinkle with half the cheese. Add tortilla chips in a layer.

3. Add rice in a layer. Drizzle with water, then sprinkle remaining cheese over the top.

4. *Bake* 10–20 minutes.

INGREDIENT	8" (1x)	10" (1.5x)	12" (2x)	14" (3x)
chicken tenders	4–6 (½ lb.)	6–9 (¾ lb.)	8–12 (1 lb.)	12–18(1½ lb.)
enchilada seasoning	1 pkt.	1½ pkts.	2 pkts.	3 pkts.
petite diced tomatoes	16-oz. can	28 oz. can	28 oz. can	28 oz. + 16 oz.
corn	8-oz. can	16 oz. can	16 oz. can	16 oz. + 8 oz.
shredded cheddar	6 oz. (1½ cups)	9 oz. (2¼ cups)	12 oz. (3 cups)	18 oz. (4½ cups)
tortilla chips	2 oz.	3 oz.	4 oz.	6 oz.
instant rice	1½ cups	2¼ cups	3 cups	4½ cups
water	1½ corn cans or 1½ cups	1 corn can or 2 cups	1½ corn cans or 3 cups	4½ (8 oz.) corn cans or 4½ cups
SERVES	4–5	6–7	8–10	12–15
CHARCOAL	16	25	36	49

★ Tortilla chips should be 2 to 2½ chips deep.

★ If too dry on top when cooked, drizzle a little water over the dry spots, cover and let stand 10 minutes.

★ GLUTEN-FREE: use gluten-free enchilada seasoning, or make your own (see Enchiladas recipe.) Make sure your tortilla chips and instant rice are gluten-free.

ENCHILADAS

1. *Preheat & Season*. *Fry* meat. Add enchilada seasoning.

2. Add soup, milk, water if it is called for, and half of the cheese. Stir.

3. Add tortilla chips and push them down into the mixture until they are covered. Sprinkle with remaining cheese

4. *Bake* 10–20 minutes.

INGREDIENT	8" (1x)	10" (1.5x)	12" (2x)	14" (3x)
ground beef	½ lb.	¾ lb.	1 lb.	1½ lb.
enchilada seasoning	1 pkt.	1½ pkts.	2 pkts.	3 pkts.
cream of tomato soup	10-oz. can	1½ (10-oz.) cans	2 (10-oz.) cans	3 (10-oz.) cans
evaporated milk	5-oz. can	5-oz. can	12-oz. can	12-oz. can
water	none	½ milk can or 5 Tbsp.	none	¼ milk can or ~6 Tbsp.
shredded cheddar	6 oz. (1½ cup)	9 oz. (2¼ cup)	12 oz. (3 cups)	18 oz. (4½ cups)
tortilla chips	2 oz.	3 oz.	4 oz.	6 oz.
SERVES	4–5	6–7	8–10	12–15
CHARCOAL	16	25	36	49

★ MEAT-FREE: for 1x recipe, use ½ cup instant rice, ½ can chili beans, and one milk can of water instead of the meat. Use 1 tablespoon less enchilada seasoning mix.

★ GLUTEN-FREE: use gluten-free soup and gluten-free enchilada seasoning, or make your own enchilada seasoning—for 1x batch, use: ¼ teaspoon cumin, ½ teaspoon garlic salt, ¼ teaspoon onion powder, dash cayenne.

HAMBURGER SOUP

1. *Preheat & Season. Fry* meat. Break into small pieces. Add onions and season generously with pepper and garlic salt.
2. Crumble crackers. Add crackers to meat and stir. Add canned goods and water. Stir.
3. *Simmer* 20–30 minutes or longer—up to one hour. Add more water as needed. Add salt and pepper as needed.

INGREDIENT	8" (1x)	10" (1.5x)	12" (2x)	14" (4x)**
ground beef	½ lb.	¾ lb.	1 lb.	2 lb.
dry onion	1 Tbsp.	1½ Tbsp.	2 Tbsp.	¼ cup
garlic salt	½ tsp.	¾ tsp.	1 tsp.	2 tsp.
crackers*	10 count	15 count	20 count	40 count
green beans	8-oz. can	15-oz. can	15-oz. can	2 (15-oz.) cans
corn	8-oz. can	8-oz. can	15-oz. can	2 (15-oz.) cans
petite diced tomatoes	15-oz. can	28-oz. can	28-oz. can	2 (28-oz.) cans
water (approximate)	1 tomato can or 2 cups	½ tomato can or 2 cups	1 tomato can or 4 cups	2 tomato cans or 8 cups
SERVES	5–7	7–9	10–14	20–28
CHARCOAL	16–18	25–28	36–39	49–53

* The crackers melt into the soup and make it thicker. For best results, use reduced fat Ritz or Townhouse style crackers.

**Fourteen-inch is 4x recipe—*Simmer* at least one hour.

★ To speed up cooking, this recipe may be done using "extra" charcoal. See page 150.

★ Best with super-lean meat or use paper towel to remove fat after frying.

★ Make sure pot is well seasoned to avoid ending up with a metallic taste in the soup.

SECTION 3: *The Recipes*

ORIENTAL FRIED RICE

1. After you *Preheat & Season*, break or cut the bacon into small pieces and add to Dutch oven. *Fry* 5 minutes. Add eggs and scramble the eggs.

2. Add water (2x the amount of eggs), peas, rice, and fried rice seasoning packets. Stir.

3. *Bake* 20–30 minutes or until rice is soft.

INGREDIENT	8" (1x)	10" (1.5x)	12" (2x)	14" (3x)
bacon (precooked)	8 slices	12 slices	16 slices	24 slices
egg product (eggs)	1 cup (4 eggs)	1½ cups (6 eggs)	2 cups (8 eggs)	3 cups (1 dozen)
peas (frozen)	1 cup	1½ cups	2 cups	3 cups
instant rice	1½ cups	2¼ cups	3 cups	4½ cups
seasoning pkts.	1½ pkts.	2 pkts.	2–3 pkts.	3–5 pkts.
water	2 cups	3 cups	4 cups	6 cups
SERVES	4–5	6–7	8–10	12–15
CHARCOAL	16	25	36	49

★ This recipe uses "same-depth" conversions. It can also be done using "maximum volume conversions" (see page 140). Bake time will be longer for maximum volume recipes in larger Dutch ovens.

★ MEAT-FREE: leave out bacon.

SHEPHERD'S PIE

1. *Preheat & Season*. *Fry* meat.

2. Add one cream soup—either cream of mushroom or cream of tomato. Add one canned vegetable—either green beans or corn. Stir.

3. Sprinkle mashed potatoes evenly over meat-soup-vegetable mixture. Do not stir. Drizzle water evenly over potatoes. Do not stir.

4. Sprinkle with cheese. *Bake* 15 minutes or until cheese is melted.

INGREDIENT	8" (1x)	10" (1.5x)	12" (2x)	14" (3x)
ground beef	½ lb.	¾ lb.	1 lb.	1½ lb.
cream soup	10-oz. can	1½ (10-oz.) cans	2 (10-oz.) cans	28-oz. can
vegetable	8-oz. can	16 oz.	16 oz.	16 oz. + 8 oz.
potato flakes	1½ cups	2¼ cups	3 cups	4½ cups
water	1¾ vegetable cans or 1¾ cups	1¼ vegetable cans of water or 2½ cups	1¾ vegetable cans or 3½ cups	2⅔ (16-oz.) vegetable cans or 5¼ cups
shredded cheddar	6 oz. (1½ cups)	9 oz. (2¼ cups)	12 oz. (3 cups)	18 oz. (4½ cups)
SERVES	3–5	4–6	6–10	9–15
CHARCOAL	16	25	36	49

★ **Do not stir potatoes into lower layer!** The recipe is meant to be layered.

★ If you notice dry spots in the potatoes when it is done, pour a little water through the cheese onto on those areas, then let stand 10 minutes with lid on.

★ GLUTEN-FREE: use gluten-free cream soup and gluten-free potato flakes.

SECTION 3: *The Recipes*

KARA'S RAZZMATAZZ

1. *Preheat & Season*. Remove pot from heat. Add fruit and vanilla pudding mix. Stir. Mixture should immediately start to thicken.

2. Add evaporated milk and first water. Return to heat and *Simmer* until mixture starts to steam. Stir constantly.

3. Sprinkle dry raspberry muffin mix over the top and drizzle with second water. Do not stir.

4. *Bake* 20–40 minutes. Dessert is done when muffin layer is lightly browned in the middle and springs back when gently touched.

INGREDIENT	8" (1x)	10" (1x)	12" (2x)	14" (3x)
crushed pineapple	8-oz. can		2 (8-oz.) can	3 (8-oz.) can
vanilla "cook & serve" pudding	3.5-oz. box		2 (3.5-oz.) boxes	3 (3.5-oz.) boxes
evaporated milk	5-oz. can		12-oz. can	12-oz. can
first water	¾ milk can or about ½ cup	Do 8" recipe	⅔ milk can or 1 cup	1 milk can or 1½ cups
7-oz. raspberry muffin mix	1 pkg.		2 pkgs.	3 pkgs.
second water	1 milk can or 5 oz.		¾ milk can or 10 oz.	1¼ milk cans or ~2 cups
SERVES	6	6	12	18
CHARCOAL	16	25	36	49

★ This is a unique and fun dessert invented by my niece when she was nine.

★ Try this in your kitchen at home: do steps 1 and 2 in a casserole dish in the microwave, then bake in the oven at 350°F.

PARMESAN PULL-APARTS

1. *Preheat & Season*. Melt butter. Remove Dutch oven from heat.

2. Break each biscuit in half and form each half into a ball. Roll the balls in the butter and arrange them in a single layer in the bottom of the pan.

3. Sprinkle with garlic salt and then with Parmesan. Slightly move rolls so the Parmesan can go down between them.

4. *Bake* 20 minutes.

INGREDIENT	8" (1x)	10" (1x)	12" (2x)	14" (3x)
butter	1/3 cube		2/3 cube	1 cube
refrigerator biscuits	16 oz.	Do 8" recipe	2 (16-oz.) cans	3 (16-oz.) cans
garlic salt	½ tsp.		1 tsp.	1½ tsp.
Parmesan cheese	3 Tbsp.		6 Tbsp.	9 Tbsp.
SERVES	5–8	5–8	10–16	15–24
CHARCOAL	16	25	36	49

SECTION 3: *The Recipes*

PEACH COBBLER

DUTCH OVEN COOKOUT, STEP BY STEP

1. *Preheat & Season*. Meanwhile, knead the butter and cake mix together in a plastic bag until a crumble forms.

2. Remove pot from heat. Add peaches with liquid to the pot. Return pot to the coals and *Simmer* until the liquid is steaming and starting to bubble. **In this recipe, it is very important for the fruit and liquid to be nearly boiling before you add the cake mix–butter layer.**

3. Sprinkle cake mix crumbles evenly over fruit. **Do not stir.**

4. *Bake* 25–45 minutes, or until lightly browned on top. Cake topping should spring back when touched (not sink in).

INGREDIENT	8" (1x)	10" (2x)	12" (3x)	14" (4x)
cake mix (French vanilla or yellow)	7–8 oz. (~2 cups) or ½ box	15–18 oz. or 1 box	22–26 oz. cake mix or 1½ boxes	32 oz. or 2 boxes
butter (2x standard amount)	²/₃ cube	1¹/₃ cube	2 cubes	2²/₃ cubes
gallon-size heavy duty zip-seal bag	1 bag	1 bag	1 or 2 bags*	2 bags*
sliced peaches	15-oz. can	2 or 3 (15-oz.) cans or 30-oz. can**	3 or 4 (15-oz.) cans or 2 (30-oz.) cans**	4 or 5 (15-oz.) cans or 2 or 3 (30-oz.) cans**
SERVES	4–5	8–10	12–15	16–24
CHARCOAL (uses "extra")	18	28	39	54

*When two bags are listed, divide butter and cake mix evenly between the bags. If your crumble starts to look like cookie dough while you are mixing it in the bag, just use your fingers to break it into small pieces and distribute the pieces evenly in a layer over the fruit.

** Each version of the recipe in the chart above can work fine with proportionally more fruit. For the eight-inch size, this is impractical since you would need an additional half can of peaches (2 cans is, in my opinion, too much). For the other size recipes though you can easily play with doing proportionately more fruit, as shown in the ingredient amounts above. For example, the fourteen-inch recipe works great with 4x of the cake mix and butter and 5x of the fruit.

★ Serve with vanilla ice cream or, if desired, serve the old-fashioned way with evaporated milk poured over the cobbler instead of ice cream.

★ This recipe can be made with almost any canned fruit or pie filling and any flavor of cake mix. Some combinations that I like include

• Sliced peaches and spice cake mix

• Canned raspberries and yellow or vanilla cake mix

• Cherry pie filling and chocolate or cherry chip cake mix. When using pie filling, use a 20-ounce can of pie filling (for the 1x recipe) and stir in 2–4 tablespoons of water after you add it to the pot in step 2 of the recipe.

★ Fresh fruit also works great for cobblers. Here are some variations:

• Fresh berry cobbler (1x version): During step 2 in the recipe, add the following to the pot: 3 cups fresh or frozen berries, 3 tablespoons sugar, ¼ cup water. **Simmer** 5–10 minutes or until liquid starts to steam and bubble. Continue with step 3 of the recipe.

• Fresh apple cobbler (1x version): During step 2 in the recipe, add the following to the pot: 5 medium apples (peeled and sliced) and ¾ cup cinnamon sugar (³/₄ cup sugar plus 1 teaspoon cinnamon.) **Simmer** 10 minutes before going on to the next step. For more of a "crisp" topping, add ³/₄ cup oats and 3 teaspoons cinnamon sugar when mixing the butter-cake mix blend.

• Fresh peach cobbler (1x version): In a separate bowl or bag, combine 3 cups (about 1 pound) sliced fresh peaches with ¼ cup sugar. Do this while your charcoal is lighting so some juice can form. Add the fruit with the liquid to the pot as instructed in step 2. If there isn't enough liquid to almost cover the peaches, add some water. **Simmer** 5–10 minutes or until peaches are heated through and liquid starts to steam and bubble. Continue with step 3 of the recipe.

STICKY BUNS

1. *Preheat & Season*. Melt butter. Remove Dutch oven from heat.

2. Break each biscuit in half and form each half into a ball. Roll the balls in the butter and arrange them in a single layer in the bottom of the pan.

3. Combine pudding mix and cinnamon sugar in a bag. Sprinkle this mixture over the top. Slightly move rolls so the mixture can go between them.

4. *Bake* 15–20 minutes.

INGREDIENT	8" (1x)	10" (1x)	12" (2x)	14" (3x)
butter	$1/3$ cube		$2/3$ cube	1 cube
refrigerator biscuits	16 oz.		2 (16-oz.) cans	3 (16-oz.) cans
butterscotch "cook & serve" pudding mix	3.5-oz. pkg.	Use 8" recipe	2 (3.5-oz.) pkgs.	3 (3.5-oz.) pkgs.
cinnamon sugar	$3/4$ cup		1½ cups	$2^1/4$ cups
zip-seal bag	quart bag		quart bag	gallon bag
SERVES	5–8	5–8	10–16	15–24
CHARCOAL	16	25	36	49

★ Cinnamon sugar = 1 teaspoon cinnamon per $3/4$ cup sugar

★ Can drizzle about 2 tablespoons water over the top (1x recipe) to help dissolve sugar mixture.

★ This recipe works fine indoors but must be made in a covered dish.

★ Even people who say they don't like butterscotch love this dish.

★ Serve the rolls piping hot. Clean the Dutch oven while it is still warm.

INTERMEDIATE RECIPES

MAIN AND SIDE DISHES

Chicken and Dumplings	74	Ranch Chicken	82
Fajitas	76	Stir Fry with Rice	83
Garden Skillet	78	Tortellini Soup	84
Lasagna	80		

BREADS AND DESSERTS

Caramel Apple Cobbler	85	Hot Fudge Cake	87
Dessert Pizza	86	Rolls	88

SECTION 3: *The Recipes*

CHICKEN AND DUMPLINGS

1. *Preheat & Season*. Place chicken, onion and carrots in the pot. Sprinkle generously with garlic salt if desired. *Fry* 10 minutes or until chicken is done. Break chicken into pieces. Transfer chicken, onion and carrots to a plate.

2. Melt butter, stir in flour. *Fry* 3 minutes. Add milk and stir until sauce is smooth. Add broth. Stir until sauce is smooth again. *Simmer* 10 minutes, stirring once.

3. Add chicken-onion-carrot mixture and frozen peas to sauce. Stir.

4. Break each biscuit in half and form into a ball. Gently set the biscuits on top of the chicken-vegetable mixture, evenly spaced.

5. *Bake* 15 minutes or until biscuits are done.

INGREDIENT	8" (1x)	10" (2x)	12" (3x)	14" (4x)
chicken tenders	4–6 (½ lb.)	8–12 (1 lb.)	12–18 (1½ lb.)	16–24 (2 lb.)
dry onion	1 Tbsp.	2 Tbsp.	3 Tbsp.	4 Tbsp.
fresh carrots, sliced or chopped	2 whole or ~1–1½ cups	4 whole or ~2–3 cups	6 whole or ~3–4½ cups	8 whole or ~4–6 cups
butter	⅓ cube	⅔ cube	1 cube	1⅓ cube
flour	¼ cup	½ cup	¾ cup	1 cup
evaporated milk	5-oz. can	2 (5-oz.) cans	3 (5-oz.) cans	4 (5-oz.) cans
chicken broth	14-oz. can	2 (14-oz.) cans	3 (14-oz.) cans	4 (14-oz.) cans
peas (frozen)	1 cup	2 cups	3 cups	4 cups
16-oz. can refrigerator biscuits	4 biscuits or 8 oz. (½ can)	1 can	1½ cans	2 cans
SERVES	4–5	8–10	12–15	16–20
CHARCOAL	16	25	36	49

★ Can leave out milk and replace with water if desired or use part milk and part water.

★ Can use chicken broth base plus water instead of canned broth.

★ If necessary, this recipe can be done using **Simmer** rather than **Bake**. The biscuits will cook in the sauce but will not get brown on top.

★ You can add extra uncooked biscuits to a batch of Parmesan Pull-aparts or Sticky Buns. All of the versions of those recipes can accommodate an extra half can of biscuits.

★ For an easy version, substitute 1 (10-oz.) can of cream of mushroom soup and 1 soup can of water for the butter, flour, broth, and milk in the 1x recipe. Skip step 2 of the recipe and just stir the soup and water in with the chicken and vegetables. Heat until steaming, then add the biscuits on top.

SECTION 3: *The Recipes*

FAJITAS

DUTCH OVEN COOKOUT, STEP BY STEP

FILLING:

1. *Preheat & Season*. **Fry** chicken. Add Fajita seasoning.

2. Add onion. **Fry** 3 minutes.

3. Add sliced pepper and diced tomato. Stir. **Fry** 3 minutes and remove from heat. Cover with foil to retain heat while you warm or cook the tortillas.

TORTILLAS:

1. Move the coals off the lid onto the foil. Support the lid upside-down over the coals. You can suspend the lid using three empty 5-oz. milk cans or similar size cans or rocks (see photo below). Use hammer and gloves for turning the lid.

2. Warm or cook the tortillas on the lid. If the lid cooks too hot, decrease the number of coals under the lid. For detailed instructions, see page 167.

SERVING:

Top the tortillas with the chicken mixture. Serve with sour cream and salsa, if desired.

Ready-to-cook tortilla on a ten-inch lid.

INGREDIENT	8" (1x)	10" (1.5x)	12" (2x)	14" (3x)
chicken tenders	4–6 (½ lb.)	6–9 (¾ lb.)	8–12 (1 lb.)	12–18 (1½ lbs.)
fajita seasoning	½ pkt.	¾ pkt.	1 pkt.	1½ pkts.
fresh onion, chopped or sliced (2x standard amount)	1 whole	1½ whole	2 whole	3 whole
red or yellow bell pepper, sliced (2x standard amount)	1 whole	1½ whole	2 whole	3 whole
fresh tomato, diced	1	1	2	3
flour tortillas	4–6	6–8	8–12	12–18
SERVES	3–4	5–6	6–8	9–12
CHARCOAL	16	25	36	49

★ Choose tortillas to fit the lid of the Dutch oven you will be using. Eight-inch precooked tortillas can be warmed on an eight-inch lid. Eight-inch ready-to-cook tortillas work best on a ten-inch or twelve-inch lid. Ten-inch ready-to-cook tortillas work best on a twelve-inch or fourteen-inch lid.

★ You can use the tortilla-cooking method in this recipe to make quesadillas. See page 167 for details.

★ GLUTEN-FREE: use gluten-free tortillas and gluten-free fajita seasoning. Or instead of fajita seasoning for 1x recipe, use: juice of one lime, ¼ cup Worcestershire sauce (gluten-free), some garlic powder, and some black pepper.

★ MEAT-FREE: double the onions, peppers, and tomatoes. Leave out the chicken.

GARDEN SKILLET

1. *Preheat & Season*. Meanwhile, prepare the vegetables. Cut the zucchini in quarters lengthwise, then slice in quarter-inch slices. Cut the corn off the cobs if using fresh corn. Cube the red bell pepper.

2. Add the butter to the pot and allow it to melt. Add all the ingredients except the corn. Cover the pot loosely with foil and *Simmer* for 5–8 minutes or until zucchini starts to look translucent.

3. Stir in corn and add salt and pepper as desired. Remove from heat. *Extinguish*. If you won't be eating right away, remove the foil and put the lid on the pot to help keep the food warm.

INGREDIENT	8" (1x)	10" (1.5x)	12" (2x)	14" (3x)
butter	1/3 cube	1/2 cube	2/3 cube	1 cube
zucchini (2x standard amount), cubed	2½–3 cups or 10–12 oz.	3–4½ cups or ~15–18 oz.	5–6 cups or 20–24 oz.	7½–9 cups or 30–36 oz.
red bell pepper, cubed	half pepper	whole small pepper	whole pepper	1½–2 whole peppers
taco seasoning *	1–2 tsp.	1½–3 tsp.	2–4 tsp.	1–2 Tbsp.
canned diced green chiles (optional)	4-oz. can	4-oz. can	2 (4-oz.) cans	3 (4-oz.) cans
fresh corn, cut off the cob or frozen corn	~1½ cups (2 cobs)	~2¼ cups (3 cobs)	~3 cups (4 cobs)	~4½ cups (6 cobs)
SERVES	3–5	4–6	6–10	9–15
CHARCOAL (uses "extra")	18	28	39	53

*amounts are non-standard amounts. The taco seasoning is meant to be a background flavor in this recipe.

★ Variation: substitute cubed garden tomatoes for the red bell pepper.
★ Serving suggestion: Make Nacho Cheese Sauce (page 55) as an appetizer. Drizzle any remaining sauce over individual servings of Garden Skillet.
★ GLUTEN-FREE: use gluten-free taco seasoning or add instead the following to the 1x recipe: 1 teaspoon garlic powder, ½ teaspoon cumin, ¼ teaspoon ground oregano.

SECTION 3: *The Recipes*

LASAGNA

1. *Preheat & Season*. *Fry* meat, if using. Add spaghetti sauce mix, tomatoes, tomato sauce, water, and Parmesan to the pot. Stir. *Simmer* 5–10 minutes or until mixture is steaming and starting to bubble.

2. Add noodles. *Simmer* 5–10 minutes more or until noodles are mostly cooked. Meanwhile, combine half of the mozzarella in a bag with the cottage or ricotta cheese.

3. Submerge spoonfuls of cheese mixture in noodles in sauce. Sprinkle the remaining cheese over the top.

4. *Bake* 15 minutes. *Extinguish*. Allow to stand covered for 15–20 minutes before serving.

INGREDIENT	8" (1x)	10" (1.5x)	12" (2x)	14" (3x)
ground beef (optional)	½ lb.	¾ lb.	1 lb.	1½ lb.
spaghetti sauce mix	½–1 pkt.	1 pkt.	1–2 pkts.	2–3 pkts.
petite diced tomatoes	15-oz. can	1½ (15-oz.) can	28-oz. can	15-oz. can + 28-oz. can
tomato sauce	8-oz. can	1½ (8-oz.) cans	2 (8-oz.) cans	3 (8-oz.) cans
water	½ tomato sauce can or ½ cup	¾ tomato sauce can or ¾ cup	1 tomato sauce can or 1 cup	1½ tomato sauce cans or 1½ cups
Parmesan cheese	3 Tbsp.	1/4 cup	6 Tbsp.	9 Tbsp. or ~½ cup
medium curly egg noodles	1/4 lb.	1/3 lb.	½ lb.	3/4 lb.
shredded mozzarella	6 oz. (1½ cups)	9 oz. (2¼ cups)	12 oz. (3 cups)	18 oz. (4½ cups)
cottage/ricotta cheese	1–1½ cups	1½–2 cups	2–3 cups	3–4 cups
heavy-duty zip-seal bag	quart size	gallon size	gallon size	gallon size

SERVES	4–5	6–8	8–10	12–16
CHARCOAL	16	25	36	49

★ It works okay to do the 3x recipe in a twelve-inch and a 4x recipe in the fourteen-inch. These might need to **Simmer** and **Bake** a little longer than indicated in the recipe.

★ MEAT-FREE: leave out hamburger. If desired, you can add (1x recipe) 1–1½ cups chopped frozen spinach to the ricotta/mozzarella mixture.

★ GLUTEN-FREE: use gluten-free noodles and gluten-free spaghetti sauce mix. Alternatively, you can substitute the following for the spaghetti sauce mix (1x recipe): 1 teaspoon garlic salt, ½–1 tablespoon basil.

RANCH CHICKEN

1. *Preheat & Season*. Melt butter.
2. Add chicken tenders to pot and toss with butter until all pieces are coated.
3. *Fry* chicken until partly done. Can break into smaller pieces with spoon if desired (depending on how you want to serve it).
4. Transfer crackers and ranch mix to a heavy-duty zip-seal bag. Crumble the crackers and mix the crumbs with the dressing mix. Pour over the chicken in the pot and toss to coat the chicken with the mixture.
5. *Bake* 15–20 minutes.

INGREDIENT	8" (1x)	10" (2x)	12" (5x)
butter	$^1/_3$ cube	$^2/_3$ cube	$1^2/_3$ cube
chicken tenders (2x standard amount)	10–12 (~1 lb.)	20–24 (~2 lbs.)	50–60 (~5 lbs.)
ranch dressing seasoning pkts.	½–1 pkt.	1–2 pkts.	2–4 pkts.
crackers	10 count	20 count	50 count
heavy duty zip-seal bag	quart size	gallon size	gallon size
SERVES	4–8	8–16	20–40
CHARCOAL (uses "extra")	18	27	39

★ Ten-inch is 2x recipe and twelve-inch is 5x. You can also make the 5x recipe in a fourteen-inch or do 3x or 4x in a twelve-inch.

★ Very tender and quick! Serve with Cowboy Potatoes and salad.

★ Variation: Use 1 head cauliflower broken into florets instead of the chicken for eight-inch recipe. Follow directions as for chicken. *Bake* 30–40 minutes or blanch ahead of time for a shorter bake time.

★ Can use slightly less ranch seasoning for milder flavor.

STIR FRY WITH RICE

1. *Preheat & Season*. Drain liquid from vegetables into the Dutch oven. Stir in stir-fry seasoning packets. Add chicken. *Simmer* until chicken is cooked and you can break it into pieces.

2. Add vegetables and peas. Sprinkle rice over the top and drizzle water over the rice.

3. *Bake* 15–20 minutes or until rice is done.

INGREDIENT	8" (1x)	10" (1.5x)	12" (2x)	14" (3x)
Chinese vegetables	16-oz. can	1½ (16-oz.) cans	2 (16-oz.) cans	3 (16-oz.) cans
stir fry seasoning	2 pkts.	3 pkts.	4 pkts.	6 pkts.
chicken tenders	4–6 (½ lb.)	6–9 (³/₄ lb.)	8–12 (1 lb.)	12–18 (1½ lbs.)
peas (frozen)	1 cup	1¹/₂ cups	2 cups	3 cups
instant rice	1½ cup	2¹/₄ cups	3 cups	4½ cups
water	1½ cups or ³/₄ vegetable can	2¹/₄ cups or 1¹/₈ vegetable cans	3 cups or 1½ vegetable cans	4½ cups or 2¼ vegetable cans
SERVES	4–5	6–8	8–10	12–16
CHARCOAL	16	25	36	49

★ In the 1x recipe you can substitute half of a sliced zucchini, 1 cup shredded carrot, or ~1 cup other vegetable for the peas. Another option is to use 1 (6–8 oz.) can sliced water chestnuts and 1 (6-oz.) can sliced mushrooms instead of the Chinese vegetables.

★ You can do the rice in a separate eight-inch Dutch oven: Use 1½ cups calrose or other oriental rice + 2 cups water. *Preheat & Season*, bring water and rice to boil, *Bake* 15 minutes. If rice seems dry, you can add a little water and let stand covered until water is absorbed.

SECTION 3: *The Recipes*

TORTELLINI SOUP

1. *Preheat & Season.* Place tortellini, tomatoes, spinach, cubed zucchini, and basil in Dutch oven. Add beef broth and water. *Simmer* 25–35 minutes. Add more water as needed

2. Remove from heat. Stir in Parmesan cheese. Serve.

INGREDIENT	8" (1x)	10" (1.5x)	12" (2x)	14" (4x)*
refrigerated cheese tortellini	9 oz. (40 count)	12 oz.	1 lb. 2 oz.	2 lb. 4 oz.
petite diced tomatoes	16-oz. can	1½ (16-oz.) cans	28-oz. can	2 (28-oz.) cans
chopped spinach	1 cup	1½ cups	2 cups	4 cups
zucchini, cubed	1½ cups	2 cups	3 cups	6 cups
basil	1 Tbsp.	1½ Tbsp.	2 Tbsp.	¼ cup
beef broth	14-oz. can	1½ (14-oz.) cans	2 (14-oz.) cans	4 (14-oz.) cans
water	~½ broth can or 1 cup	~¾ broth can or 1½ cups	~1 broth can or 2 cups	~2 broth cans or 4 cups
Parmesan	3 Tbsp.	¼ cup	6 Tbsp.	¾ cup
SERVES	4–5	6–8	8–10	12–16
CHARCOAL	16	25	36	49

*The fourteen-inch recipe is 4x and may take a little extra time to heat through. You can also do 3x in a fourteen-inch

★ Can substitute 2 cups frozen "California blend" mixed broccoli, cauliflower, and carrots for the zucchini. Can substitute fresh baby spinach or chopped Swiss chard for the frozen spinach.

DUTCH OVEN COOKOUT, STEP BY STEP

CARAMEL APPLE COBBLER

1. *Preheat & Season*. Meanwhile, mix sour cream and pound cake mix in bag. Set aside.
2. Peel and slice apples. Mix with cinnamon sugar and water in Dutch oven. *Simmer* 10 minutes.
3. Remove apples from heat. Stir cook & serve pudding mix into the apples. Spoon or squeeze cake mix over the top of the apples. Do not stir.
4. *Bake* 20–40 minutes.

INGREDIENT	8" (1x)	10" (1.5x)	12" (2x)	14" (3x)
heavy duty zip-seal bag	quart or gallon bag	gallon bag	gallon bag	gallon bag
sour cream	8 oz. (1 cup)	12 oz.	16 oz.	1½ lb.
16-oz. pound cake mix	½ box	¾ box	1 box	1½ boxes
apples	4–5	6–7	8–10	12–15
cinnamon sugar	¾ cup	¾ cup	1½ cups	2¼ cups
water	½ cup	¾ cup	1 cup	1½ cups
butterscotch "cook & serve" pudding mix	3.5-oz. pkg.	3.5-oz. pkg.	2 (3.5-oz.) pkgs.	3 (3.5-oz.) pkgs.
SERVES	4–5	6–8	8–10	12–16
CHARCOAL	16	25	36	49

★ When you mix the pound cake mix and sour cream, the mixture will be very thick—almost like cheesecake.

★ You can substitute 2 ounces of freeze-dried apple slices for the fresh apples in the 1x recipe. Double the amount of water.

★ Variation: Don't do the cake part. Serve the caramel apple sauce over vanilla ice cream.

SECTION 3: *The Recipes*

DESSERT PIZZA

1. *Preheat & Season*. Melt butter. Add cake mix. Stir until crumbles form. Use a spoon to remove about a quarter of the crumbles onto a plate.

2. Distribute the remaining crumbles evenly in the bottom of the pot and press them down to form a crust.

3. *Bake* 20 minutes or until crust begins to brown around the edges, then spread pie filling over crust. Sprinkle remaining crumbles over pie filling. *Bake* 10–15 more minutes or until crumbles start to brown. *Extinguish*. Allow pizza to cool with lid on for 10–15 minutes before serving. Serve warm.

INGREDIENT	8" (1x)	10" (1.5x)	12" (2x)	14" (3x)
butter	$^2/_3$ cube	1 cube	$1^1/_3$ cubes	2 cubes
French vanilla cake mix or other flavor	7–8 oz. or $^1/_2$ box	12 oz. or $^3/_4$ box	16–18 oz. or 1 box	24 oz. or $1^1/_2$ boxes
20-oz. pie filling—any flavor	$^1/_2$ can	$^3/_4$ can	1 can	$1^1/_2$ can
SERVES	4–5	6–8	8–10	12–16
CHARCOAL	16	25	36	49

★ Variation—S'mores Pizza: Leave out pie filling. For 1x recipe sprinkle crust with ~1/3 cup mini chocolate chips and ~1 cup mini marshmallows. *Bake* as directed. Serve warm.

HOT FUDGE CAKE

1. *Preheat & Season*. Meanwhile, mix chocolate cake mix with evaporated milk in zip-seal bag and set aside.

2. Pour water into the preheated Dutch oven. When the water is steaming and bubbling, stir in chocolate frosting. Cover lightly with foil and *Simmer* until mixture starts to steam and bubble. **Make sure water-frosting mixture is nearly boiling before you add the cake mix.**

3. Tear or cut off a corner of the bag and squeeze cake mix over the hot frosting mixture in a layer. Do not stir.

4. *Bake* 20–40 minutes. Serve with vanilla ice cream.

INGREDIENT	8" (1x)	10" (2x)	12" (2x)	14" (3x)
heavy duty zip-seal bag	quart size		gallon size	gallon size
evaporated milk	5-oz. can		2 (5-oz.) cans	3 (5-oz.) cans
chocolate cake mix	7–8 oz. or ½ box	Use 12" recipe	16–18 oz. or 1 box	24 oz. or 1½ boxes
water	2 milk cans or 1¼ cups		4 milk cans or 2½ cups	6 milk cans or 3¾ cups
chocolate frosting	8 oz. or ½ can		16 oz. or 1 can	1½ lb. or 1½ cans
SERVES	5–7	10–14	10–14	15–22
CHARCOAL (uses "extra")	18	27	39	53

★ This delicious recipe has moist cake on top with hot fudge sauce underneath!

★ Betty Crocker Rich & Creamy frosting recommended.

★ Use the other half can of frosting to make s'mores—spread the frosting on a graham cracker and add a toasted marshmallow.

★ You can also do the 3x recipe in a twelve-inch and a 4x recipe in a fourteen-inch. It will take longer to *Bake* and you may need to add new charcoal partway through.

SECTION 3: The Recipes

ROLLS

1. *Preheat & Season*. Melt butter in the Dutch oven pot. Remove the pot from the heat. Coat each roll in butter and position the frozen rolls in the pot in a single layer.

2. Place the lid on the Dutch oven but remove the coals (*Extinguish* or use them to cook something else). Let the rolls rise in the warm Dutch oven for one hour.

3. 20–30 minutes into the rise time, light new coals to use to bake the rolls.

4. *Bake* 20–40 minutes.

INGREDIENT	8" (1x)	10" (1.5x)	12" (2x)	14" (3x)
butter	$1/3$ cube	½ cube	$2/3$ cube	1 cube
freezer rolls	10	12–15	20	30
SERVES	5–10	6–12	10–20	15–30
CHARCOAL	16 +16	25 + 25	36 + 36	49 + 49

★ In cold weather, you will need to leave a few coals on the lid of the pot or do something to insulate the pot or else it will cool down too quickly and the rolls won't rise.

★ In pleasant or warm weather do not allow the rolls to rise more than 1½ hours —they will rise too much.

★ If desired, you can make the rolls like Parmesan Pull-aparts or Sticky Buns. Just add the other ingredients at the end of step 1 in the Rolls recipe.

SECTION 4:

The Whys behind the Hows

• •

THE WHYS BEHIND THE HOWS			**91**
DUTCH OVENS			**93**
Selecting	93	First-time Seasoning Methods	101
Dutch Oven Rehab	96	Dutch Ovens: General FAQs	105
Getting Ready to Season	99	Dutch Ovens: Cleaning FAQs	115
MAKING YOUR OWN DUTCH OVEN KIT			**121**
COOKOUT FOOD			**131**
Food Safety	132	Food FAQs	144
Converting Recipes	135		
CHARCOAL AND OTHER FUEL			**149**
Charcoal Review	149	How Weather Affects	
Amount of Charcoal	150	Charcoal	154
Lighting a Second Batch of		Making Treated "Easy-light"	
Charcoal	153	Charcoal	154

Reusing Extinguished
   Charcoal   155
Emergency Charcoal
   Lighting   157

Cooking with Fire   157
Cooking over a Butane Stove 165
Fuel Section—FAQs   170

PLANNING FOR GROUPS   180

Checklists   181
Leave No Trace   187

Quiz   189
Conclusion   191

THE WHYS BEHIND THE HOWS

Once you have the needed ingredients and supplies, you can successfully cook great food in a Dutch oven using just the Steps in section 2 and the instructions in your recipe. When it comes to helping others learn though, I think it is much easier if you understand how this method works and why I recommend doing certain things one way as opposed to another. Section 4 is all about these hows and whys.

If you are going to be teaching this method, reading this section is a must! But even if you are just cooking for yourself or your family, knowing the whys behind the how can make you feel more confident and more able to tweak the method and recipes to suit your own tastes.

After you read this section, you will know things that even experienced Dutch oven cooks don't know—or only know instinctively. If you are teaching the method to others, this information will put you in a position to answer most of the questions your group members may ask. But most important, reading this information will help you understand the process on a deeper level—and you will be the expert!

The topics covered in this section are, for the most part, the same topics you encountered in section 1: "Getting Ready," but with much more detail. In this section you will find in-depth information on:

- **DUTCH OVENS**
- **MAKING A DUTCH OVEN KIT**
- **FOOD**—including food safety and how to use your Dutch oven indoors
- **FUEL**—including details about charcoal and information about other fuel sources you can use.

The final part, "Planning for Groups," gives you checklists and tools for using *Dutch Oven Cookout: Step by Step* with large groups, especially youth groups in a campout setting.

Here's what can happen when you start using *Dutch Oven Cookout: Step by Step* (done in the style of the well-loved book *If You Give a Mouse a Cookie* by Laura Joffe Numeroff):

IF YOU WANT TO BECOME AN EXPERT . . .

If you pick a recipe and work through the Steps, you might find that you can Dutch oven cook!

If you can Dutch oven cook, and people eat your yummy food, they might ask you to teach them.

If others ask you to teach them, they might start asking you Dutch oven questions that start with "Why . . ."

If they ask you Dutch oven questions that start with "Why . . ." you might decide to read all of section 4.

If you read all of section 4, you will become an expert!

If you become an expert, more people will want you to teach them.

If more people want you to teach them, you might decide to give them a copy of the book.

If you give them a copy of the book, they might pick a recipe and work through the Steps.

· DUTCH OVENS ·

In this book when I say "Dutch oven," I am referring to a cast iron cooking pot with legs and a tight-fitting rimmed lid. The kind of Dutch oven I mean can also be called a "camp oven."

The term "Dutch oven" can also refer to an indoor roasting pot, sometimes cast iron, often enameled. That's not the kind of pot I'm talking about; however, if you are looking to borrow a Dutch oven from someone, it's a useful distinction to be aware of. When I was a teenager, a friend offered to lend me a Dutch oven for use on a camping trip. Imagine my disappointment when my friend opened her truck to reveal . . . an indoor Dutch oven—no legs, no rimmed lid. We made do, but it was a bit more difficult.

SELECTING A DUTCH OVEN

If you are shopping for a Dutch oven, I recommend purchasing one or more of the eight-inch or two-quart size, rather than a bigger size. Cooking with eight-inch Dutch ovens have several advantages:

★ They are easier to carry, season, clean, and store, whether you are using them indoors or out.

★ Cooking times can be shorter.

★ Smaller amounts mean no leftovers if you are cooking for a small group—something especially helpful if you are camping.

★ Using several small Dutch ovens lets you do a variety of recipes when cooking for a group. It makes it easier to accommodate picky eaters or dietary needs.

★ It allows more people to have a hands-on experience—better for learning and more fun.

★ Your initial investment is less—if you sale-shop, you may be able to get an eight-inch Dutch oven for less than $20. (Try shopping at farming supply stores or discount outdoor stores.)

If you normally cook out with 3 to 6 people, two eight-inch Dutch Ovens would be a great start for you. The cost should be about the same or less as getting one twelve-inch Dutch oven and you can make about the same amount of food, but you will have more options. For example, you can cook two different main dishes, or cook one main dish and one dessert then supplement your main dish with a salad or another pre-done side dish.

If you are usually cooking out with more than 6 people—and having each person involved isn't an issue—you may want to consider starting by buying a twelve-inch Dutch oven. Main dish recipes in this book for the twelve-inch generally feed 8 to 15, and you can make a dessert to feed up to 24.

SOME MORE THINGS TO KEEP IN MIND

★ Most boxes are labeled with the lid diameter of the Dutch oven and the number of quarts it holds. Be careful not to confuse the two—an eight-inch Dutch oven holds about two quarts. An eight-quart Dutch oven measures about fourteen inches. There is a big size difference!

★ Some Dutch ovens come in "standard" and "deep" sizes,

and some brands are just extra deep to begin with. For the recipes in this book, I strongly recommend getting Dutch ovens that are comparable to the standard-depth Dutch ovens from Lodge. The reasons for this and more information can be found in the section, "Converting a Regular Recipe to a Dutch Oven Recipe," page 138. As a point of reference, a standard twelve-inch Lodge Dutch oven holds about 6 quarts (deep holds 8 quarts.) A standard fourteen-inch Lodge Dutch oven holds 8 quarts (deep holds 10 quarts.) See also photo, page 142.

★ Many Dutch ovens sold currently come "preseasoned." This means that a seasoning coat has already been applied in the factory. With a preseasoned Dutch oven, you are ready to go straight to The Cookout Steps. If you purchase a Dutch oven that is not preseasoned (or have a new nonpreseasoned Dutch oven sitting around at home), go to page 101 for directions on first-time seasoning. There are several seasoning methods to choose from, each with its own advantages, so choose the one that is most convenient for you.

★ If your Dutch oven is old or you got it used, it may need some TLC before you cook in it. Use the chart on the next page to decide what it needs. One of the easiest ways to rehabilitate a Dutch oven is to simply put it in a self-cleaning oven, run the clean cycle, and then re-season from scratch. However, unless it is really, really rusty or gunky, I suggest trying one of the following methods first.

DUTCH OVEN REHAB

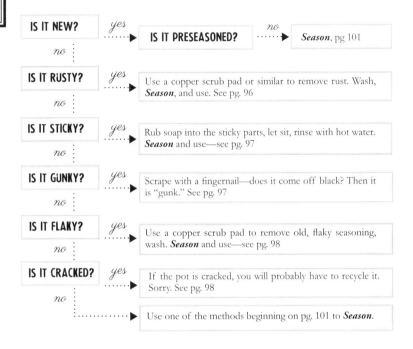

| IS IT NEW? | *yes* → | IS IT PRESEASONED? | *no* → | *Season*, pg 101 |

IS IT NEW? *yes* → **IS IT PRESEASONED?** *no* → *Season*, pg 101

no

IS IT RUSTY? *yes* → Use a copper scrub pad or similar to remove rust. Wash, *Season*, and use. See pg. 96

no

IS IT STICKY? *yes* → Rub soap into the sticky parts, let sit, rinse with hot water. *Season* and use—see pg. 97

no

IS IT GUNKY? *yes* → Scrape with a fingernail—does it come off black? Then it is "gunk." See pg. 97

no

IS IT FLAKY? *yes* → Use a copper scrub pad to remove old, flaky seasoning, wash. *Season* and use—see pg. 98

no

IS IT CRACKED? *yes* → If the pot is cracked, you will probably have to recycle it. Sorry. See pg. 98

no → Use one of the methods beginning on pg. 101 to *Season*.

RUSTY: If your Dutch oven has patches of flaky rust, remove the rust with steel wool or a copper scrubber (see photo), rinse, dry, and immediately season. If the rust is just a little discoloration (no flakiness), you can just wash the rust out of the pot using hot water, dry the pot thoroughly, and then season it.

STICKY: If the Dutch oven was oiled but not properly seasoned and washed before being stored, it may be sticky. This is due to the oil going rancid. To remove the stickiness, rub concentrated liquid dish soap (not dishwasher soap, just soap for hand-washing of dishes) into the sticky layer and let it sit for 30 minutes or so. Scrub lightly with a damp, non-abrasive scrubbing pad, then rinse the Dutch oven in hot water. Repeat as needed, then season. If the stickiness isn't too extreme, you can bake the Dutch oven in an oven or on a gas grill at 500 degrees. It is done when a metal utensil scraped across the surface doesn't leave a mark.

GUNKY: Scratch the surface of the Dutch Oven with your fingernail (the inside of the lid is a good place to try this.) If there is black "gunk" that comes off on your fingernail, your Dutch Oven is "gunky." Gunk comes from built up food residue (turned mostly to carbon) or from layers of grease or oil mixed with ash. Gunk doesn't taste or look good in food and it doesn't have nonstick properties. There are a couple ways to remove the gunk:

> *Method 1:* Scrape as much as you can off with a pot scraper, then rub liquid soap (without water) into the remaining gunk. Rinse with hot water while rubbing with a dishcloth or non-abrasive scrubbing pad. When no gunk comes off and the surface feels relatively non-greasy, you are done. Dry the Dutch oven with a paper towel.

> *Method 2:* Place the Dutch oven over a heat source (a few briquettes or a stove burner on medium works well) with the lid on so the lid gets warm too. When the Dutch oven and lid are warm, wipe them with a dry paper towel. The

paper towel will probably come out black. Keep wiping until no more black comes off. Add a little oil and wipe again. Continue until the paper towel doesn't come out black. Turn up the heat and finish by seasoning the Dutch oven.

FLAKY: If Dutch oven gets too hot or the oil was applied in too thick of a layer when it was seasoned, the seasoning can start to flake off. Scrub with a copper scrubber or with steel wool until all the black flakes are removed. Wash with soap and water, then re-season, or follow Method 2 under "Gunky." (Note: Flaking can also occur if you don't get the wax factory coating completely removed from your new Dutch oven before you season it.)

CRACKS: Sometimes you will find an old Dutch oven or other cast iron pan or pot that has a hairline crack. The danger in using a cracked Dutch oven is that water could seep into the crack, expand into steam, and cause the pot to break apart. Theoretically, that is what could happen, but it isn't something I've been able to test! Still, it's not a good idea to use a Dutch oven with a crack—in terms of physical safety or food safety. If you have a local metal recycling

company, they will be happy to take it off your hands.

DENATURED: This happens rarely, but it can happen—if a Dutch oven or other iron pot overheats, the metal can convert to a different oxidation state. When this happens, the metal itself turns red. You can tell it isn't rust because a damp paper towel wiped over it doesn't come out rust-colored. If parts of a Dutch oven overheat and the metal becomes denatured, the seasoning coat will most likely flake off those areas and the metal itself will have a mottled look (see photo.) In all but the most severe cases, you can apply a new seasoning coat and continue using the Dutch oven; however, the seasoning coat may not adhere as well to the denatured parts.

GETTING READY TO SEASON

If your Dutch oven is new (but not preseasoned), wash the Dutch oven in mild dish soap and hot water before you start—often there is a light layer of wax on the Dutch oven to protect it during shipping. Use a soft bristle brush to get into the small spaces around where the handle attaches. If the pot seems exceptionally rough, you can try to smooth it a little using a copper scrubber or wire brush (cheaper brands sometimes have a rougher surface).

To oil an eight-inch Dutch oven, inside and out, you will need approximately 1 teaspoon vegetable oil (see chart below for other sizes). The first time you season the Dutch oven, the rough iron surface may cause your paper towel to tear. If this is a problem, you can try using a soft rag. After the initial coats, the surface will be smoother. The first time you season you may also need slightly more oil than the amounts given in the chart below. As stated in the **Setup** Step, you should use as much oil as will stick to the Dutch oven without creating puddles.

After you apply the oil, use one of the following seasoning methods (page 101–104) to get your Dutch oven ready for cooking.

DUTCH OVEN SIZE	8"	10"	12"	14"
amount of oil needed	1 tsp.	1½ tsp.	2 tsp.	3 tsp.
just inside	½ tsp.	¾ tsp.	1 tsp.	1½ tsp.

After you have seasoned several times, you can choose to season just the inside of the pot during the **Preheat & Season** Step. If you do this, you will need about half the usual amount of oil. Over time, you will probably need to season the inside of the pot and the outside of the lid more frequently than the outside of the pot and the inside of the lid. The outside of the lid needs frequent seasoning for protection from rust (in case of rain) and because the heat from the charcoal can burn the seasoning coat off. The inside needs constant reseasoning to maintain the nonstick coating and also to prevent rust.

TAKE NOTE!

Whenever you finish seasoning a Dutch oven, you should either cook in it or wash it before putting it away. No matter how good the seasoning method you use, there will almost always be a little oil left that did not completely convert to seasoning. By washing the Dutch oven with hot water and mild soap after you season, you ensure that the oil is washed away and so the Dutch oven will not become sticky during storage.

Charcoal Method

You will need the following amounts of pretreated charcoal, depending on the size of your Dutch oven:

DUTCH OVEN SIZE	8"	10"	12"	14"
amount of charcoal	16 + 4	25 + 5	36 + 6	49 + 7

1. Oil the pot and lid and set up charcoal on the Dutch oven lid, on foil, as directed in the cookout steps—***Step 1: Setup***. When you are done, go on and do ***Step 2: Light***.

2. When the coals are lit, spread them out on the lid as directed in ***Step 3***. If the coals won't fit in a single layer on the lid, do two layers of coals around the edges or keep a few to the side to add as the coals on the lid burn and get smaller.

3. Place the pot over the coals and ***Preheat & Season*** for 30–40 minutes, swiping the inside of the Dutch oven with an oily paper towel whenever it starts to look "dry."

4. When the coals start to cool down, do ***Step 6: Extinguish***. ***Clean*** the Dutch oven before putting it away.

PROS: Doesn't take any advance prep. Assuming you have what you need to wash off the wax coating, you can do everything at your cookout site, while cooking another meal, if desired.

CONS: The bottom of the pot will (at first) have a harder and darker

SECTION 4: The Whys behind the Hows

seasoning coat than the sides. Also the oil on the top of the lid may burn away from the long-term contact with the coals. This isn't really a problem though since you will season it each time you use it for cooking.

Stovetop Method

You can do this seasoning method on a glass-top, gas, or spiral-burner stove.

Note: extensive testing has been done of this method on several kinds of stoves without any noticeable wear or harm to the various types of burners; still, be safe and use caution.

1. Lightly oil pot and lid. Set pot on burner with lid on, lid slightly ajar. Select a burner that is close to the same size as the Dutch oven you are seasoning. If using a spiral burner, make sure the legs of the Dutch oven are balanced evenly on the coil.

2. Turn on heat. Start with burner on medium and gradually increase heat to find the right temperature for your stove (you may want to make a note of this setting, since it will be the same as your **Preheat & Season** or

Simmer setting when doing indoor Dutch oven cooking. See Using Your Dutch Oven—Indoors!, page 137.) As the oil starts to bake on, it should smoke slightly, but not to the point that it sets off your smoke alarm!

3. After the oil has baked on (about 15–20 minutes), you can continue adding coats of seasoning by swiping the inside or outside, pot or lid, with an oily paper towel, adding a little oil as needed.

PROS: Easy to apply lots of coats, one after the other, especially to the inside surfaces. Also you can keep track of exactly what is going on.

CONS: Takes more monitoring during the process and is not as good for large Dutch ovens. Also, you may want to consider doing the lid in the oven while you are doing the pot on the stove since the lid will not get as hot using this method.

· ·

Oven Method

1. Coat all surfaces lightly with cooking oil, and place the lid (right side up) and the Dutch oven (upside down) on the oven shelf.

2. Bake at 375°or 400° until the oil has dried or baked on (about an hour).

3. Add another light coating of oil and bake again.

PROS: Easy; produces good, consistent results.

CONS: Can make your kitchen a little smoky. If you use the higher temperature, you will get a darker, harder coat, but it will produce a significant amount of smoke when you open the oven door.

Gas Grill Method

Follow same instructions as for seasoning in the oven. Turn on grill, close lid, season on high for about an hour, repeat.

PROS: Will produce results most like the factory preseasoning, and it doesn't smoke up your house.

CONS: Not everyone has a gas grill.

· DUTCH OVENS: GENERAL FAQ'S ·

★ EVERYONE TALKS ABOUT SEASONING A DUTCH OVEN. WHAT DOES THAT MEAN?

Seasoning happens when oil is applied to an iron or aluminum surface and then heated. When intense heat is applied, the molecular structure of the oil changes. With enough heat, a smooth, hard nonstick coating is created. When first seasoned, a cast-iron Dutch oven will be light or dark brown and have a smooth, hard coating. If the Dutch oven is sticky or oily to the touch, more heat needs to be applied to complete the molecular transformation. Several coats of seasoning applied one over the other will make the surface of your Dutch oven even smoother. Over time, the color of the seasoning will turn black.

★ WHAT DOES THE SEASONING COAT DO FOR THE DUTCH OVEN? WHY IS IT IMPORTANT?

The seasoning coat turns a cast iron pot—prone to rusting and hard to clean—into a sleek, extremely versatile nonstick pot.

★ WHY IS IT IMPORTANT TO PREHEAT THE DUTCH OVEN?

The main reason is that preheating significantly enhances the nonstick qualities of your Dutch oven. In side-by-side tests, food

SECTION 4: *The Whys behind the Hows*

sticks noticeably less in ovens that are preheated. Preheating also sanitizes the oven and releases odors.

★ I HAVE A BRAND NEW DUTCH OVEN. DO I NEED TO DO ANYTHING TO IT BEFORE I USE IT?

The answer to this depends on how long you have had it and what kind of pot you acquired. Many cast iron Dutch ovens now are sold "preseasoned." This means that a seasoning coat was created in the factory, before you received it. In this case, you don't need to do anything but wash it with mild soap and water and start following the steps. If you have an older Dutch oven or a non-preseasoned Dutch oven, follow the instructions for washing and seasoning at the start of this section.

★ HOW DO DIFFERENT BRANDS OF DUTCH OVENS COMPARE?

I have successfully used several different brands. I have found though that Dutch oven shape and volume can vary considerably between brands, even when you are getting the same "size." For example, an eight-inch from Lodge (one of my favorite brands) has a total interior volume of about 2 quarts and 1 cup, while an eight-inch from Texsport is slightly taller and narrower and has an interior volume of 2 quarts and 2 cups. An eight-inch from a manufacturer called Old Mountain that I have only seen occasionally has an interior volume of 7 cups, which is a little small for most of the recipes in this book. While different brands of Dutch ovens vary in quality control during manufacturing, I feel that for the beginning Dutch oven cook it is just fine to buy whatever you find on sale. That being said, I use Lodge as my standard Dutch oven and so do many other people. Because of that I would recommend comparing whatever oven you plan to buy to a lodge Dutch oven of the same diameter. In other words, if you are looking at an eight-inch Dutch oven of brand X, make sure it seems to have roughly the same volume and shape as an eight-inch from Lodge. Another thing to look at is the finish of the metal. Lodge Dutch ovens tend to be slightly smoother, so it is a little less hard on your paper towel when you are applying the oil for seasoning.

★ I WANT TO LABEL MY DUTCH OVEN SO IT DOESN'T GET MIXED UP WITH OTHERS. IS THERE A GOOD WAY TO DO THIS?

Labeling your Dutch oven is a good idea. One of the easiest ways is to go to a key shop and get a brass tag on a split ring labeled with what you want it to say. Get matching tags for the lid and the pot so you can keep them together.

★ **YOU RECOMMEND USING THE EIGHT-INCH SIZE. WHAT ARE THE PROS AND CONS OF THE OTHER SIZES?**

- *Twelve-inch:* This is a good size if you are consistently cooking for a group of 6–14 people—it is basically equivalent to a 9 x 13 pan and holds 2x the base recipe for most of the recipes in this book.

- *Fourteen-inch:* This is the size commonly used in situations where a guide (such as, on a river trip) is doing all the cooking for a large group. Using a fourteen-inch requires more strength and longer arms. It is awkward to season indoors; it will however fit in most ovens. In my experience, when a fourteen-inch is used in a youth setting, the leaders do all the cooking. I like using the fourteen-inch when I need to do dessert for a large group (it can serve up to 36) or when I need to do an easy main dish for a large group. I also use it when doing some advanced recipes, outside the scope of this book. It holds 3x the base recipe in this book.

- *Ten-inch:* This size seems like it would be a nice medium size, but it is a difficult size for adapting recipes. This is because it holds 1.5 times the base recipe in this book or .75 times a household recipe designed for a 9 x 13 pan. This means that when you try to do a recipe in this book using a ten-inch Dutch oven, you will often end up with half a can of this or that left over (if you multiply by 1.5). When you try to do a standard household recipe in a ten-inch, the recipe may end up too deep in the pot, changing the end result and possibly affecting quality. (For more information, see Converting Recipes in this Book for Regular Kitchen Use, page 135.)

109

★ SOME PEOPLE I KNOW LINE THEIR DUTCH OVEN WITH FOIL BEFORE COOKING IN IT. SHOULD I DO THAT?

Please don't. It can cause some big problems. It is nearly impossible to line a Dutch oven with foil without getting at least a pinhole leak in the foil. If you are cooking something sweet like a cobbler, liquid containing sugar is almost certain to end up between the foil and the pot. When you go to take out the foil, the foil will be glued to the pot, the sugars will have turned to sticky carbon, and cleaning the pot becomes much more difficult. Another problem is that the lid generally does not fit as well or as tightly on a pot lined with foil. This can lead to longer cooking times. One of the main reasons people put foil in is because they think it will make it easier to clean, but if you have preheated and seasoned, you will not have any problem cleaning the pot, especially if you clean it while it is still warm. It is now possible to buy aluminum liners to fit some sizes of Dutch ovens. These are made from thicker aluminum and are already formed to the right shape, so it is less likely for them to get a hole in them. There are probably specific situations where these liners would be useful, but I'm not sure exactly what those situations would be since the food will brown and cook differently in a liner than in the actual Dutch oven. Recently, some camping supply stores have been selling circular pieces of baking parchment designed for use in Dutch ovens.

These are less prone to leak or tear than foil, and, I think, have a better chance of giving you good results than a foil liner. I would use parchment in situations when cleaning your Dutch oven is difficult or impractical or when you want to be able to lift your food out of your Dutch oven.

★ WHAT HAPPENS IF I APPLY TOO MUCH OIL WHEN SEASONING A DUTCH OVEN?

If excess oil is allowed to puddle during *Preheat & Season* or when you season your Dutch oven for the first time, the oil can still turn into a hard coating, but it may start to flake off after use. Please see "Dutch Oven Rehab" at the start of this section.

★ SOME PEOPLE SAY IT IS BETTER TO USE SHORTENING FOR SEASONING A DUTCH OVEN AND SOME PREFER OIL. IS THERE A REASON TO USE ONE OR THE OTHER?

Oils that are liquid at room temperature have a molecular structure that lends itself more readily to the cross-linking transformation that happens when heat is applied during seasoning. It is also easier to dispense oil into the Dutch oven and easier to see right away if you have gotten too much (see previous question).

★ IS THERE A TYPE OF OIL THAT IS BETTER TO USE?

In reality, any vegetable oil will work. In theory, polyunsaturated oils have the molecular structure most susceptible to cross-linking. Safflower, sunflower, and soybean oils all contain high amounts of polyunsaturated oil molecules. These oils are, however, also the most susceptible to going bad with time. If you keep any kind of oil in your Dutch Oven Kit, I recommend dumping it out and replacing it with new once during the year. It also helps to store your oil in a cool location.

★ DO I NEED TO SEASON THE DUTCH OVEN AFTER I CLEAN IT?

When you are done cooking in your Dutch oven, it is fine to repeat the *Preheat & Season* step if you want to. However, this takes more time and heats the Dutch oven up again at the time when you want it to cool down so you can put it away or pack it up. You also have to keep your charcoal going longer, which means your extinguishing can will still be hot when you want to pack up. You will also need to wash the pot again after you season to get rid of any residual oil that didn't turn into seasoning. For more detail, see the next two questions.

SECTION 4: *The Whys behind the Hows*

★ I'VE HEARD YOU SHOULD ALWAYS OIL THE DUTCH OVEN AFTER YOU USE IT. IS THAT TRUE?

It is better *not* to oil the Dutch oven after you clean it—the coat of seasoning you put on it during the Preheat & Season Step will protect the surface while it is stored. A seasoning coat is created when oil and heat are applied. Oiling the Dutch without heating it can result in dirt sticking to the surface, and the oil can turn rancid and sticky during storage. For more detail, see the next question.

★ I'VE HEARD THAT YOU SHOULD OIL THE DUTCH OVEN BEFORE YOU PUT IT AWAY AND THAT AS LONG AS YOU USE JUST A THIN COATING OF OIL, IT SHOULDN'T GO RANCID DURING STORAGE. IS THIS TRUE?

No. Whenever vegetable oils are exposed to the oxygen in air, they will go rancid. Going rancid means that the oil develops an off flavor or odor and becomes sticky. You may have noticed this process going on around the neck of the bottle of vegetable oil in your kitchen. The drips around the neck are in a thin layer, and therefore exposed to more oxygen than the oil in the bottle. With time, the oil around the neck turns rancid and becomes sticky or gummy. This is what happens to any coat of vegetable oil that you spread on your Dutch oven but do not convert right away to a seasoning coat by the application of intense heat. When oil is kept cool, it goes rancid more slowly, but if the oil is in a thin layer (even contained in plastic and kept cool) it will start to go rancid within a matter of days. Another word for going rancid is oxidize, and it is similar to what happens to iron when it rusts or to a pencil eraser when it starts to get hard.

★ WHY DO MOST OTHER BOOKS SAY TO OIL THE DUTCH OVEN BEFORE PUTTING IT AWAY?

I think this tradition was passed down from the pioneers and ranchers. In those days people were using their Dutch ovens daily. Usually they would use them in the morning for breakfast and then use them again in the evening for supper. In this kind of situation, there was no time for the oil to go rancid between uses and the extra coating of fresh oil would help ensure that the pot would not rust if the weather turned rainy.

★ IF I AM GOING TO BE STORING MY DUTCH OVEN FOR A FEW MONTHS, IS THERE ANYTHING SPECIAL I SHOULD DO BEFORE PUTTING IT AWAY?

Not really. Just put a paper towel inside it and store it in a dry location. Do not oil it before putting it away for storage.

★ CAN I USE AN INDOOR DUTCH OVEN FOR OUTDOOR COOKING? CAN I USE MY CAMPING DUTCH OVEN FOR INDOOR COOKING?

A small (eight- to twelve-inch) outdoor Dutch oven works great in an indoor oven or on the stove (See Using Your Dutch Oven—Indoors!, page 137 for more detail.). Cast-iron Dutch ovens designed for indoor use can be used outside, but you have to improvise a rim around the lid to contain the coals on and legs to hold up the pot. It is really much easier to use an outdoor oven indoors than the other way around.

★ I GOT AN OLD DUTCH OVEN AT A YARD SALE. HOW DO I MAKE IT READY TO USE?

Before you buy, check that the pot and lid do not have any hairline cracks. If the pot is not cracked and the lid fits well, chances are it will make a great Dutch oven. Please see "Dutch Oven Rehab" at the start of this section.

★ I'VE HEARD THAT YOU SHOULD NEVER POUR COLD WATER INTO A HOT DUTCH OVEN. IS THAT TRUE?

In theory, very cold water, poured into a very hot pot could cause the pot to crack. In practice, time after time of testing, I've never had a preheated pot crack from adding cold water.

★ I'VE HEARD I SHOULD NEVER USE SOAP IN MY DUTCH OVEN. WHY DOES THIS METHOD SAY IT IS OKAY?

Strong detergents could strip away part of the seasoning coat of the Dutch oven, but mild dish soap will not. To prove this to yourself, try using mild dish soap to remove grease or oil that has baked onto the edges of an old cookie sheet and turned yellow or black— it is nearly impossible to remove! That is the same type of coating that you have created on your Dutch oven through seasoning it. The good news is that soap will remove oils that have not baked on or that were only partially converted to a seasoning coat. This is a good thing, since those oils, if not removed, can quickly turn sticky or rancid.

★ I'VE HEARD IT'S NOT GOOD TO USE WATER IN A DUTCH OVEN. IS IT OKAY TO USE WATER? WHY?

Almost all food contains some amount of water—if you cook in a Dutch oven, you are in essence putting water in it. Water in a Dutch oven is only a problem if the Dutch oven does not have a good seasoning coat or if water is allowed to stand in it for several days or weeks. By following the ***Preheat & Season*** step each time you use your Dutch oven, you should develop of good coat of seasoning that will thoroughly protect the iron

SECTION 4: The Whys behind the Hows

from rust. If your seasoning is a little thin in places, you may see small rust spots after you do the ***Clean*** steps. If you do, simply wipe away the rust and season well before the next use.

★ I'VE HEARD YOU CAN CLEAN YOUR DUTCH OVEN WITH SALT AND OIL OR SAND AND WATER. WHAT ABOUT THESE METHODS?

Salt and oil can be a good alternative in situations where water is scarce, but it can lead to sugars being left behind and converting to sticky carbon when the Dutch oven is heated again. Once converted to carbon, food particles are nearly impossible to remove without starting your seasoning process again from scratch. Natural sand (like from a river bank) contains organic particles that can act like a mild soap, therefore this can be quite an effective method of cleaning as long as the sand is damp or used with some water.

★ WHAT ABOUT USING FIRE TO BURN OUT THE DUTCH OVEN AFTER USE?

Some people will invert the Dutch oven over a fire to "clean" it after use. This method has several disadvantages:

1. It may remove the seasoning coat—unevenly or all together.

2. It tends to bake sugars from the food onto the pot.

Baked-on sugars turn to carbon and can be very difficult to remove.

3. It can take a long time (if you leave it on long enough to do anything).

4. It can leave a thin coat of smoke or soot that can discolor or leave off-flavors in your food the next time you cook.

★ WHAT SHOULD I DO IF I HAVE PROBLEMS GETTING THE DUTCH OVEN CLEAN?

Put hot or boiling water in the Dutch oven and allow it to soak, up to 24 hours if necessary. If there is still food stuck on, try simmering the water. If that doesn't work, you may have to try some of the methods in the Dutch Oven Rehab section.

★ SHOULD I DO ANYTHING DIFFERENT WHEN I CLEAN MY DUTCH OVEN INDOORS?

When using my Dutch oven indoors, I clean it the same way I clean my nonstick pans—using a gentle kitchen brush, hot water, and mild dish soap. I find that if I am using hot water on a well-seasoned Dutch oven, I can actually let the pot air-dry upside-down in a draining rack. I usually use a paper towel to hand dry the top of the lid to make sure all the groves around the letters, rim and handle get dry quickly.

★ WHAT IF SOMETHING HAPPENS, AND I DON'T GET A CHANCE TO CLEAN THE DUTCH OVEN RIGHT AWAY?

It's easier to clean the Dutch oven while it's warm, but as long as you have a well-seasoned Dutch oven, it actually works fine to clean it even a day or two later. Before you leave it, remove all food, scrape it, and leave the lid off so the food residue will dry out. When you go to clean it, fill the pot with hot water and some soap, let it soak for a few minutes, and then scrub it.

★ I'VE HEARD YOU SHOULD NEVER PUT A DUTCH OVEN IN A DISHWASHER. WHAT HAPPENS IF YOU DO?

I tried it once because I was curious. Basically, the strong detergent and dishwasher action stripped off any part of the seasoning coat that hadn't turned dark brown or black. The Dutch oven I washed ended up with a few mildly rusty parts. I wiped the rust off and re-seasoned with no permanent damage done. It really is just easier to wash it by hand, but it won't ruin your Dutch oven if you decide you want to try it.

★ DO I NEED TO CLEAN THE DUTCH OVEN EVERY TIME I USE IT?

The answer to this might seem obvious, but it isn't. There are actually recipes where the food comes out so cleanly that all you need to do is wipe the inside of the oven out with a dry paper towel. This is usually true when you cook rolls or cornbread. One caution: if you decide not to wash, make sure there is no food stuck on and not too much residual oil. If there is food stuck on, and you go to use the oven again, the stuck-on food can end up encased in the oil you apply in Step 1 and will burn on when you *Preheat & Season*. Food burnt on in this manner can become hard to remove or can turn into "gunk." (See "Dutch Oven Rehab," page 97.) You also don't want to leave oils leftover from cooking in the pot because they can go rancid in storage.

★ IT SEEMS LIKE I AM USING A LOT OF PAPER TOWELS? IS THERE ANYTHING I CAN DO TO MINIMIZE THAT?

Let me walk you through what I do, step-by-step. I open the Dutch oven that has been stored with a paper towel inside. I use that towel to oil the Dutch oven in Step 1. I keep that towel, setting it to one side (preferably in a location where it won't get dirty, blow away, or ruin something else because it has oil on it.) I use that towel again when I *Preheat & Season*. After *Preheat & Season*, I don't throw the towel away; I keep it and use the non-oily part to wipe my fingers if they get goopy, if I spill food where I don't want it, or to get food residue off the serving spoon when I am ready to *Clean*. During the *Clean* step, I use a new towel to dry the Dutch oven. If the oven is twelve-inch or larger, I might need two towels. If I *Clean* while the oven is warm, and let the water drip out of the oven when I pour out the cleaning water, I only need one towel. When I'm ready to put the oven away, I put a clean towel inside which will become towel number one the next time I cook. In total, each time I cook, I use 2 square towels per Dutch oven (sometimes 3 if the Dutch oven is large).

· MAKING YOUR OWN DUTCH OVEN KIT ·

If you bargain shop or are able to use some things you already have, you should be able to put a kit together for around $40–$50. For any project, having the right tools in the right place is half of the work. By putting together a Dutch Oven Kit once, you can save yourself having to gather up what you need every time you cook out.

What to look for in selecting items for your Dutch Oven Kit:

★ **TOOL BOX** Look for one 18 to 20 inches long, heavy duty plastic (see photo on page 13). If you sale-shop, you might find one for $8–$15. (The Home Depot's orange "Homer Box" is inexpensive and can work well.)

★ **COOKING / SERVING SPOONS** Material should be wood or plastic so you don't damage your seasoning coat without meaning to. As for the shape, a flat bottom edge allows you to more easily break up meat as it cooks or serve up the last gooey goodness of a cobbler. I like to use the types of spoons pictured here. I get mine at the local dollar store or at Ikea.

★**BIODEGRADABLE SOAP** Look for small bottles of camp soap in camping supply stores. You can also use a mild liquid dishwashing soap like Dawn. I use soap that is blue or green rather than yellow so I don't mix it up with the oil.

LIQUIDS IN YOUR KIT

I keep the soap and oil in the upper tray of the tool box so that if either leaks, the mess is contained. Even small changes in altitude or temperature can cause any kind of liquid to leak. I generally keep a folded paper towel under my liquids to help soak up any leaks. You can also squeeze out as much air as possible before closing the lid—this helps maintain the seal and will help prevent leakages if you change altitude.

★**OIL** You can use vegetable oil of any kind. I keep mine in a small bottle with a flip-top lid, similar to the 3-oz. bottles sold for travel liquids. I recommend using a small container for two reasons: (1) so that if it leaks or spills it doesn't ruin your whole kit and (2) because oil will go

rancid after a while and will need to be replaced. I recommend dumping out your remaining old oil and replacing it with new once a year.

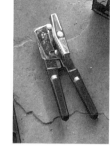

★ **CAN OPENER** Buy a can-opener for your DOK—don't just try to remember to take yours from home. The last thing you want is to be camping and not be able to get into your canned goods! My favorite brand is Swing-A-Way. Although it is one of the least expensive brands, it is the most durable brand I have found.

★ **POT SCRAPER** Pot scrapers can be hard to find. Look for them near the cash register at kitchen supply stores or in the grocery store. It is worth some work to find one—they make clean-up so much easier!

★ **FIR OR SPRUCE CONES** Pick them up in the forest or in your neighborhood or yard. They are generally between 1 and 3 inches long and have flexible "bristles," not hard like the traditional pine cone. When they are damp, the bristles are closed. When I gather cones, I usually pick up a bagful to keep at home and then add more to my DOK as they are used up. (Questions about what the fir cones are for? Please see *Step 7: Clean*, page 35.)

★**MATCHES** I keep matchboxes with wooden matches inside a waterproof plastic box. The container shown here was a "first aid kit" container from a dollar store. A long-handled lighter is also a good option.

★**SALT AND SPICES** I keep salt, pepper, garlic salt, and cinnamon sugar in my kit. Select salt and pepper shakers that are plastic, not cardboard, so that they will not be affected by dampness or leaks in the kit.

★**PARING KNIFE** Some of the intermediate recipes call for chopped fresh vegetables. You can prepare these ahead, or pack a paring knife in your kit. If you decide you want one in your kit, don't just put in one that you don't like—using a dull knife can be frustrating when you are out in a camping environment!

★**LITTLE EXTRAS** I recommend putting in a pair of scissors or kitchen shears. These can come in very handy for opening bags. I especially like to use them for cutting up precooked bacon to use as a recipe ingredient. Measuring spoons or cups and a vegetable peeler can also come in handy. If you like to make foil dinners when you camp, you could also put in a permanent marker. If everyone writes their name on their foil dinner before it goes into the fire, it makes things simpler later on. I also recommend putting in a few extra quart or gallon zip-seal bags in case you forget to pack one for mixing recipe ingredients.

★**HAMMER** The hammer makes a great lid-lifter—the best in fact. It doesn't have to be a particularly expensive or heavy hammer (dollar store hammers work fine if you can find them), but it must have a curved claw. You may see fancy Dutch oven lid-lifters advertised, but most of them will not fit inside your kit and won't work nearly as well (please see photos). If you are buying a hammer at a hardware store, select one that weighs 10 or 12 ounces.

A) single-hand lift of an eight-inch lid; B) double-hand lift of a twelve-inch lid. Using a hammer as a lid lifter as shown keeps the lid from wobbling and allows you to hold it sideways. This comes in handy for dumping ashes off the lid.

★**FOIL** A twelve-inch roll of household weight aluminum foil works fine for most applications in this book. If you cook in twelve- or fourteen-inch Dutch ovens a lot, you probably will want to have a roll of extra-long,

heavy-duty foil. It won't fit in your kit, but it works better for the Steps when you work with large Dutch ovens.

★**PAPER TOWELS** Any kind of paper towels can be used, but I prefer ones that tear off in squares instead of half-sheets. You really need a full square for applying the oil in *Step 1*. A good trick is to leave the plastic wrapping on the roll of towels and remove the cardboard roll from the center of the towels by making a small hole in the plastic at one end. You can then dispense the towels from the center of the roll. This keeps the towels clean and dry and prevents them

from unrolling all the way down the hill! It can be tricky removing the cardboard center, so try different brands of towels. Some brands (often the cheaper ones) have less glue in the center. Work slowly, twisting the tube until it starts to come out.

★**GLOVES** a pair of cloth or leather work gloves will protect your hands from heat when carrying the Dutch oven or the extinguishing bucket by the handle.

★**TONGS** Use long metal tongs for moving charcoal briquettes. Light duty tongs work fine for this (but don't let anyone try to use your tongs as a lid lifter!).

★ **ASH BRUSH** This brush is used for brushing ashes off the outside of the Dutch oven, especially the lid. A cotton dish mop or natural bristle long-handled scrubbing brush both work fine. Keep it dry, for use with ashes only.

★ **GARBAGE BAGS** I always have a few draw-string kitchen garbage bags in my kit. I like the drawstring kind because you can hang the bag up from one of the drawstrings and still have the bag open enough for people to put their garbage in. Having a garbage bag set up at the start of your cookout encourages people to clean up after themselves.

★ **EMERGENCY LIGHTING STICKS** These are small fire-starting sticks (such as these made by Diamond) that you can use to get your charcoal lit when all else fails! See "Emergency Charcoal Lighting" on page 157 for more information.

★ **EXTINGUISHING BUCKET** This doesn't actually go in your Dutch Oven Kit, but it is an important part of your equipment. The easiest place to find new gallon paint cans is in the paint section at your hardware store. Often these will have an interior coating of grey primer. This primer will probably peel off during your first uses of the bucket. If this happens, don't re-use those coals, just discard them (after they are cold.) I usually buy my buckets from an industrial container supply company. They sell metal pails that don't have any coating.

Tips for Cleaning Your Dutch Oven Kit

★ **CAN OPENER**—crank a paper towel through the gear and blade (as if you were opening a can) after each use or as often as needed. If the cutting blade has become sticky, use a damp paper towel and then a dry one. The cutting blade of a can opener is prone to rust; keep it clean and dry and it will last longer.

★ **UPPER TRAY**—run through the top rack of a dishwasher. If sticky or oily residue remains, rub straight dish soap into the sticky area (rub it in like lotion) then clean with very hot water and a scrubbing brush. If your tray still seems sticky, try spraying it with WD-40, rubbing it with a rag or paper towel, and washing again.

★ **SPOONS, SCRAPER, KNIFE**—run through dishwasher every now and then. Replace spoons if they become too scratched or melted.

★ **GLOVES AND ASH BRUSH**—wash in a mesh bag in a washing machine. Use mild soap, gentle cycle.

★ **HAMMER**—lightly oil the head with mineral oil or WD-40 if it starts to show rust stains.

Dutch Oven Kit Inventory

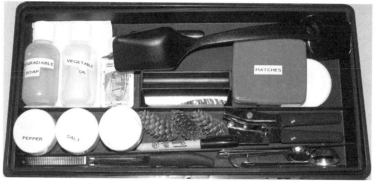

Above: Dutch Oven Kit Tray; Below: Dutch Oven Kit Base

★ BASE:

- hammer/lid-lifter
- leather gloves
- long metal tongs
- foil

- paper towels
- ash brush
- garbage bags
- fire starters

★ **TRAY:**

- Dutch Oven Cookout: Step-by-step
- cooking spoons (plastic or nylon)
- can opener
- matches or lighter
- plastic pot scraper
- biodegradable soap
- vegetable oil
- soft fir cones (for cleaning)
- salt & pepper
- other seasonings: (garlic salt, cinnamon sugar, and so on)
- paring knife

★ **EXTRAS:** *you may also want:*

- kitchen shears
- cutting board
- vegetable peeler
- spoons for tasting
- measuring spoons or cups
- extra zip-seal bags
- extra-long heavy-duty foil
- flashlight or headlamp
- hand sanitizer
- permanent marker

· COOKOUT FOOD ·

As mentioned in Section 1, the recipes in this book are designed to:

★ be easy to take camping

★ be nearly impossible to burn

★ be made in several standard Dutch oven sizes

★ guarantee that the meat gets cooked to safe temperatures

★ use no dishes other than the Dutch oven

★ require very little knife use

★ include gluten-free and vegetarian options

★ be as fool-proof as possible

They were also designed (in combination with the cookout methods) to follow HACCP guidelines. Haven't heard of HACCP? Unless you are a health inspector or food service manager, you probably haven't. The idea behind HACCP is that you analyze every part of a recipe—from the point where the ingredients come in your door to the point where the food is set on the table—for what could go wrong. Then you take steps to make sure nothing does go wrong, at least with respect to food safety. I won't bore you with the details of how the recipes and methods fit into HACCP or what the CCPs are, but if you are familiar with the HACCP guidelines, you will notice them as you work through the steps and recipes.

When you go about analyzing a recipe for what could potentially go wrong, there are several factors that come into play. The most obvious one is heat—too much and you have hockey puck rolls (something I have personally made at least once in my life), too little and you end up with raw meat. In this Cookout Food section I will suggest some ways you can keep your cookout food safe—from start to finish—and also go into more detail on how heat affects the food in these recipes. This will include how to make these recipes indoors without using a Dutch oven, how to make these recipes indoors *using* a Dutch oven and how to convert your own recipes for a Dutch oven.

ACKNOWLEDGMENT: While all the recipes in this book were either invented for this book or adjusted for use with this method, the ideas had their roots in many different sources. I'd like to acknowledge all who contributed by giving ideas, testing recipes, and giving feedback on the recipes (you know who you are), but especially my husband, my favorite "guinea pig."

FOOD SAFETY

As a certified food manager, I spent quite a bit of time thinking about keeping food safe to eat, especially in the camp setting. A few of the most important food safety principles include:

★ Avoiding cross-contamination (for example, not getting raw meat juices on something like a salad)

★ Keeping hot foods hot and cold foods cold

★ Cooking meats to correct internal temperatures

★ Avoiding bare-hand contact with food that is ready to be

eaten (this helps prevent the spread of viruses and other pathogens)

The recipes in this book are designed to make it easy to observe safe cooking practices—even out of doors. For example, in this book, the recipes all call for meats to be cooked before other ingredients are added. There are some great recipes out there for cooking a whole chicken in a Dutch oven with potatoes and carrots (a personal favorite) and many recipes that involve larger cuts of bone-in meat with other ingredients. These can be executed safely and well, but they involve longer cooking times, more charcoal, and more experience. I would categorize them as "Advanced" recipes— something to try once you have the method down and feel like being adventurous with your cooking.

The ingredients in the Standard Ingredient List tend to be foods that either require no refrigeration, or can easily be frozen (with a few exceptions). This makes it easier to "keep cold foods cold." One of the great properties of Dutch ovens is that they keep food warm for some time, even after the heat source is extinguished, thus making it easier to "keep hot foods hot."

The lists on the following pages give some further ideas for keeping food and people safe at your cookout.

Storing and Transporting Food

★ Prepackage meats in bags containing the correct amount for a given recipe so you don't have to handle it—just dump it in.

★ Freeze any foods that can be frozen so they will stay cold longer. For instance, meats—chicken, beef, and others freeze very well and will stay frozen for several hours even if you are not taking a cooler.

★ When packing an ice chest, pack uncooked foods in a separate ice chest from ready-to-eat foods to prevent cross-contamination. Pack foods you intend to use first near the top and food you plan to use later near the bottom.

★ When hiking or camping, use foods that won't keep as well earlier in the trip than foods that will keep longer. Keep in mind that foods that are dry, salty, or acidic keep longer than other foods.

Preparing food

★ Avoid getting meat juices on your hands. Wash your hands or use hand sanitizer if you have to handle meat.

★ Don't lick your fingers or cooking utensils—it spreads germs and could make you sick!

★ Don't use a knife that was used to cut raw meat for cutting something that won't be cooked.

★ Make sure vegetables or fruits to be eaten raw have been thoroughly washed.

★ Keep hot foods hot and cold foods cold. This means keeping hot foods above 140° F and cold foods below 40° F. If you plan to keep leftover hot food, get it cooled to below 40° F within a few hours. Put cold items away as quickly as you can after use.

★ Cook meats before adding other ingredients. Hint: Usually chicken breast or chicken tenders can't be broken up with a cooking spoon as called for in the recipes unless it is nearly cooked through.

Cleaning Up

★ Make a place for garbage before you start cooking so you can clean up as you go along. This makes cleanup easier at the end and helps prevent attracting insects or animals.

★ Make sure to take all garbage with you when you leave a cookout site. Leave the site cleaner than you found it.

★ Put garbage in a covered, animal-proof trash container. Recycle anything you can and stack or crush disposable cups or other containers before you throw them away so they will take up less room.

CONVERTING RECIPES

One of my requirements in writing this book was that the method should be flexible. This section is all about the flexible ways to use the recipes—converting the recipes in this book for use in your kitchen, using your Dutch oven indoors, and converting your own recipes for use with this method.

Converting Recipes in This Book for Regular Kitchen Use:

While I always tell people that this book is more about the method than about the recipes, I get excited about the recipes too!

They aren't gourmet recipes like "Pheasant with Truffles," just great easy recipes for everyday—and they work well indoors as well as outdoors. I often give this book to college students who are moving out because the recipes are simple, the ingredients are easy to keep on hand, and, if you make the 1x recipe, you don't end up with way too much food for one or two people. You don't need much cooking skill to figure out how to make these recipes indoors with normal kitchen pots and pans, but here are a few tips to make it easier:

★ Read the recipe instructions through carefully. If you are using a recipe that says **Fry** and then **Bake**, you will need a frying pan to fry in and a casserole dish or baking pan to bake in. If the recipe says **Simmer** you will probably need to do all or part of the recipe in a saucepan or deep sauté pan on the stove. If you are making the eight-inch recipe, you will need an eight- to ten-inch frying pan for the **Fry** step and a two-quart casserole dish or 8 x 8 baking pan for the **Bake** step. You would need a two-quart saucepan for **Simmer**. If you are making a double recipe (2x), you can use a 9 x 13 pan or casserole dish for the **Bake** step.

★ With some recipes, you can do the **Fry** step in a casserole dish in the microwave, add the other ingredients, and then transfer the casserole dish to your preheated oven—this saves you having to wash the frying pan!

★ For most dishes that need to **Bake**, you can set your oven to 350°. For cobblers and desserts that call for extra charcoal, you should set your oven to 375°.

★ Use common sense and experiment a little and you will soon know the easiest recipes by heart!

Using Your Dutch Oven—Indoors!

You can also make all of these recipes indoors using your outdoor Dutch oven, especially the eight-inch size. When using your outdoor Dutch oven inside, you do the first few steps over your stove, do the **Bake** step in your oven, and then you can do cleanup using your own sink! Cooking with your outdoor oven indoors is a great way to practice your Dutch oven cooking skills, it is a good alternative when the weather is bad, and, if you want to try one of your own recipes in a Dutch oven, it provides a more controlled environment for testing. You can use any kind of stove—gas, electric, or glass-top, just be gentle with your stove and use common sense. (See also "First Time Seasoning Methods—Stovetop," page 102, and "Oven," page 103.)

Here are step-by-step instructions:

1. Lightly oil the inside of your eight-inch, ten-inch, or twelve-inch Dutch oven and lid. If your recipe has a **Bake** step, preheat your oven and place the Dutch oven lid in the oven while you preheat the pot on the stove. For most recipes you will preheat to 350°. For recipes that call for extra charcoal, you will preheat to 375°. If your oven has a "Roast" setting you can use that instead of your bake setting to better simulate cooking outdoors with charcoal.

2. Set the Dutch oven pot over the burner (make sure the legs are stable) and turn the burner on to high or medium-high. On a scale of 1–10, you will usually need an 8, depending on the size of the Dutch oven with respect to the size of the burner.

SECTION 4: The Whys behind the Hows

3. Allow time for the pot to **_Preheat & Season_**. If the oil starts to smoke excessively, turn the burner down slightly and use that lower setting the next time. **_Fry_** at the same temperature. **_Bake_** by transferring the Dutch oven pot to the oven and putting the preheated lid on the pot. Be careful not to tip the pot too much as you find a place for the legs to go through the slots in your oven rack. Make sure the Dutch oven is centered in your oven. If desired, you can take the lid off for the last 10 minutes or so of cook time to allow for better browning of the food.

4. When cleaning a well-seasoned Dutch oven indoors, use warm water, soap, and a dishcloth or non-abrasive scrubber. Dry the Dutch oven with a towel when you're done, or heat it up a little to dry it, and then store it with a dry paper towel inside. Tip: Don't leave a Dutch oven soaking in an enamel sink—rust from the bottom of the legs could stain your sink.

Converting a Regular Recipe To a Dutch Oven Recipe:

After you have made several recipes in this book and have become comfortable with the method, you may decide to try to make some of your own recipes in a Dutch oven. There are several types of "indoor" recipes that convert well for use with this step-by-step method in a Dutch oven. These include recipes for casseroles, soups, and some dessert and breakfast recipes. If the casserole or dessert recipe you want to convert makes enough for a 9 x 13 pan, then half of that recipe will fit in an eight-inch Dutch oven and can become your base recipe.

DUTCH OVEN SIZE	8"	10"	12"	14"
If recipe fits a 9 x 13, multiply by this amount	.5	.75	1	1.5

Note: the measurements in this chart are based on Lodge brand Dutch ovens, but several other brands have comparable dimensions.

By using this conversion chart, your prepared food will end up approximately the same depth as the original recipe. Having a converted recipe the same depth as the recipe you are converting can be critical for achieving similar results. (See "Brownie Analogy" on page 143.) While having a recipe the same depth is often very important, there are also recipes where depth doesn't really matter. Here are some examples of each type:

Depth Does Matter:

★ When the dish is layered. if your pan is proportionately too big, you might not have enough of a certain ingredient to make a complete layer. If your pan is too small the layers may end up too thick, in which case it is nearly impossible to serve it in such a way that everyone gets part of each layer. Example: Shepherd's Pie

★ When the recipe is dense and moist. If the food is too thick, it will take much longer to bake and may come out very different than you expect. The edges may burn before the center gets done. Example: Fourth of July Cake

★ When the recipe is cooked like a stir-fry. If the vegetables to be cooked are stacked up too deep in the pan, they will end up being stewed in their own juices instead of sautéed and the end result will be very different. Example: Fajitas

Depth Doesn't Much Matter:

★ When the recipe is something runny like soup. The properties of the liquid allow for a different kind of heat distribution so that all parts can become evenly heated without any part burning. Example: Taco Soup

★ When a dense moist recipe is something that can be stirred partway through. Example: Cheesy Chicken

★ When a cake or biscuit layer on top is cooked partially by boiling liquid from below. Example: Hot Fudge Cake

★ When there is room for movement of hot air around the food inside the Dutch oven. Example: Ranch Chicken

When you have the kind of recipe where having the same depth doesn't much matter, you can convert the recipe just based on volume, if desired. The charts below recaps how to convert recipes for various Dutch oven sizes while maintaining the same depth (for recipes where it matters) and shows how to convert just based on volume (for recipes where it doesn't matter.)

SIZE OF OVEN: DIAMETER	8"	10"	12"	14"
Typical interior Dutch oven depth	3"	3¼"	3 3/4"	3¾"
Same-depth recipe	1x	1.5x	2x	3x
FEEDS	3–5	5–7	6–10	10–15

SIZE OF OVEN: VOLUME	2 qt.	4 qt.	6 qt.	8 qt.
Maximum volume recipe	1x	2x	3x	4x
FEEDS	3–5	6–10	9–15	12–20

The thing that is really cool about same-depth recipes is that (amazingly enough!) if you use the charcoal amounts indicated for each size in the charcoal section (page 150), the recipe takes almost the exact same amount of **Bake** time in a fourteen-inch regular depth Dutch oven as it does in an eight-inch! This is because the food is the same thickness, and the amount of coals called for is proportional to the area of the Dutch oven.

1)Coals lighting simultaneously on an eight-inch lid and a twelve-inch lid. 2) Both cakes are baking. 3) Both cakes are brown on top and are done in middle at the same time.

There is just one main exception: as mentioned previously, some Dutch ovens come in regular and "extra deep." When you **Bake** a same-depth recipe in an extra-deep Dutch oven, the coals on top are enough further away from the top of the food inside the Dutch oven that the food cooks much slower and often doesn't turn out as well because it is not cooking at the correct temperature for that food. Extra-deep Dutch ovens will work fine for foods that are cooked with **Fry/Simmer** only, but I don't recommend using them for same-depth baked recipes.

Dutch Ovens and Depth: Dutch ovens generally get bigger in diameter with increasing size, but only slightly deeper. Shown left to right: an eight-inch Dutch oven (3 inches deep), a ten-inch Dutch oven (3 1/4 inches deep), a twelve-inch Dutch oven (3 3/4 inches deep) and fourteen-inch "extra deep" Dutch oven (5 inches deep). A regular fourteen-inch Dutch oven is usually 3 3/4 inches deep. The Dutch ovens shown come from a variety of manufacturers.

If you convert a recipe using the volume conversion in the table on page 141, the recipe may take a little longer to cook and, in some cases, this could mean you would need to light a second batch of charcoal. This is covered in more detail on page 151 and page 153.

BROWNIE ANALOGY

Keeping food the same depth when you increase or decrease a recipe can be very important for getting the expected results. Here are some examples to illustrate this point:

Example A—different size, same depth: You bake a 9 x 9 pan of brownies and a 9 x 13 pan of brownies in your oven at home. They take about the same amount of time to bake and when you try a brownie from each pan they are similar in texture.

Example B—too deep: Now imagine you mix up some brownie batter and pour it into a bread pan with the batter twice or three times as deep as the batches in example A. It would take much longer for these brownies to bake. In fact, even if baked four or five times longer than the other batches, they would still not be done. Even if they did eventually get cooked through, they would have a different texture than the brownies in example A.

Example C—too thin: You mix up another batch of brownie batter and spread it very thinly in a large pan to bake. These brownies would end up dry and might burn around the edges.

· FOOD SECTION—FAQS ·

★ WHAT IS THE PURPOSE OF THE STANDARD INGREDIENT LIST?

The Standard Ingredient List gives the amounts needed for each ingredient when used in the base (1x) recipe. I think it keeps things simpler when you know that every recipe will take certain can sizes or a certain amount of a given ingredient. If you are measuring out the food for multiple meals at once, this can really help. The Standard ingredient List also gives more detailed information about each ingredient. Because of this, I like to take a copy of the Standard Ingredient List with me when I go shopping. Even if I have made a detailed shopping list, sometimes running through the Standard Ingredient List helps me remember something I randomly left off my shopping list.

★ IN SOME OF THE RECIPES, THE TWELVE-INCH VERSION IS 2X AND IN SOME IT IS 3X. WHY IS THAT?

Some recipes cook better if they are always the same thickness. Those recipes are 2x in the twelve-inch version. Some recipes cook fine regardless of how thick they are. Those recipes are often 3x in the twelve-inch version. For more detail on this, see Section 4: Converting a regular recipe to a Dutch oven recipe, page 138.

★ I'VE HEARD DUTCH OVENS WILL ABSORB FLAVORS FROM FOOD OR SOAP AND PASS THOSE FLAVORS ON. SHOULD I WORRY ABOUT THAT?

The iron of the Dutch oven is porous and will absorb odors, but these are released when the oven is preheated. If you sniff the oven while you are preheating you might be able to determine which recipe was last made in that Dutch oven! As the Dutch oven gets hotter, that smell will go away and be replaced by the subtle smell of hot, fresh oil.

★ I'VE HEARD THAT COOKING ACIDIC FOODS IN A DUTCH OVEN CAN BE PROBLEMATIC. WHAT'S THE SCOOP ON THAT?

It is true, acid reacts with iron. When it does, you end up with a metallic taste in the acidic food. If your Dutch oven has a good seasoning coat, the acid in acidic food can't come into contact with the metal. If you feel your Dutch oven isn't well coated, or if you cook a more acidic food like Taco Soup and end up with a metallic taste, you probably want to season more thoroughly or at a higher temperature before making that recipe again.

★ I ACCIDENTALLY STIRRED THE CAKE MIX INTO THE FRUIT WHEN I WAS MAKING COBBLER. WHAT CAN I DO?

Unfortunately, not a lot. I have found that no matter how long I cook this kind of disaster, it doesn't really change consistency. You can try serving it up as a "cake mix smoothie" (it doesn't have any raw egg, so it's okay to do this), but you probably won't get many takers.

★ CAN I SUBSTITUTE REGULAR MILK FOR EVAPORATED MILK IN THE RECIPES?

If you are adding water at the same time as the evaporated milk, you could substitute regular milk for the milk + water amount. If there is no water being added with the evaporated milk, it is important to use evaporated milk. Evaporated milk has slightly higher protein content than regular milk and this does make a difference in how certain recipes turn out.

★ CAN I SUBSTITUTE CANNED CHICKEN FOR FROZEN CHICKEN IN THE RECIPES?

In most recipes you can; a 13-oz. can works well for the base recipe. You would simply ignore the **Fry** step and go straight to **Bake**. I would probably not use canned chicken for the recipes in the Intermediate section though unless it was an emergency. You could also experiment with using canned beef in some of the recipes that call for ground beef. Ground beef substitutes such as flavored TVP can also work out okay in some of the recipes that call for ground beef.

★ I FOLLOWED THE INSTRUCTIONS, BUT MY RECIPE IS BROWN ON TOP AND TOO GOOEY STILL IN THE MIDDLE. WHAT SHOULD I DO?

This can happen. Here are a couple different options to fix it: Option one is to extinguish half the coals on the lid and leave the food baking for another 15–30 minutes with fewer coals. Option two would be to just let it keep baking. You would only do this if the coals are already less than half of their original size. Once coals have been reduced to half of their original diameter, they put out considerably less heat.

★ I MADE A BATCH OF CORNBREAD AND IT WASN'T ALL EATEN. CAN I KEEP IT IN THE DUTCH OVEN OVERNIGHT AND EAT IT FOR BREAKFAST?

Yes . . . and no. In terms of food safety, it is okay to leave things like rolls, cornbread, or Fourth of July Cake in your Dutch oven overnight. My one recommendation is that you leave the lid off of the Dutch oven until the food is completely cool. If you don't, steam from the food can condense on the underside of the lid. If your seasoning coat is a little thin, a small amount of rust can form and rusty water can drip down on your food. I also wouldn't do it in an area where the outside temperature will remain above 65 degrees overnight. I don't recommend storing any food in your Dutch oven that has a higher water content than the recipes mentioned.

★ I ONLY HAVE AN EXTRA-DEEP DUTCH OVEN IN THE SIZE I WANT TO USE. CAN I STILL MAKE SAME-DEPTH RECIPES?

Yes, but you will need more charcoal on top—approximately three to five coals per three-quarter inches of extra headspace inside the Dutch oven. (See also table on page 150.)

★ DO CROCK POT RECIPES CONVERT WELL FOR USE IN A DUTCH OVEN?

When you first think about it, it seems like they would. The reason they don't usually convert well is that the recipes in this book are relatively quick cooking—that is, they only have to bake for 20–40 minutes—and they all bake at a relatively high temperature. Most crock pot recipes cook for at least 2–3 hours at a low temperature. It is possible to do a crock pot recipe in a Dutch oven, but to achieve the same or similar results you would have to use less charcoal so that the cooking temperature would be lower, and *Bake* for a much longer period of time. This would mean lighting a second, and probably a third batch of charcoal. (See also page 153, "Lighting a Second Batch of Charcoal.")

· CHARCOAL AND OTHER FUEL ·

No matter where, when, or what you cook, cooking by definition takes fuel or an energy source of some kind. For the step-by-step method, I prefer pretreated charcoal since it is easy to use. In this section I will go over information relating to charcoal, but also discuss other fuels you can use outdoors such as fire and butane stove.

Charcoal Review

Just a reminder—to follow the Cookout Steps, you will need charcoal briquettes that are:

1. High quality (don't go for the store brand—they don't work as well)

2. Weigh about one ounce each (don't go for "extra large")

3. Are pretreated (Matchlight or other easy-light charcoal)

You can make your own pretreated charcoal—this is explained later in this section. It is a good idea to count your charcoal out into heavy duty zip-seal bags before your cookout. There are several reasons for this:

- It saves time at your cookout site.
- It keeps the charcoal dry in damp weather.
- You can dump your charcoal straight out onto the lid, and then build your pyramid using tongs. This means you don't have to get your hands all sooty if you don't want to.
- It makes it easy to marinate your own charcoal.

- You don't have to haul charcoal that you aren't going to use to your cookout site.

Amount of Charcoal

Every Dutch oven book seems to have a slightly different chart for how many charcoal to use for different sizes of Dutch ovens. For the recipes in this book, I recommend a certain amount of charcoal per square inch of lid. The math behind this is explained in "The Math of Charcoal," page 151. The basics of what you need to know though are in the chart below. When you are doing the *Fry/Simmer* step, you will have the total count of charcoal under your Dutch oven, as explained in the Steps. When doing the *Bake* step, you will keep most of the coals on the lid and arrange a few under your Dutch oven (exact numbers are given below). Some of the recipes call for "extra charcoal." For these recipes you use the extra charcoal under your Dutch oven during *Fry/Simmer* and on the lid during *Bake*.

DUTCH OVEN SIZE (LID DIAMETER)	8"	10"	12"	14"
Number under pot during Bake	4	6	9	12
Number on lid during Bake	12	19	27	37
TOTAL COUNT OF CHARCOAL	**16**	**25**	**36**	**49**
"extra" charcoal	2	2–3	3	3–4
APPROXIMATE NUMBER OF POUNDS OF CHARCOAL NEEDED	1	1½	2½	3

The easy way to remember the numbers in this chart is the following: Total number of coals = half of the lid diameter times itself. (In other words, the radius squared. For more info, see "The Math of Charcoal" below.) When arranging the charcoal, I like to arrange the coals under the pot in a ring just smaller than the base of the pot. On the lid I generally put a solid ring of charcoal around the edge and then distribute the rest in a checkerboard pattern over the remaining part of the lid.

As explained on pages 141–142, same-depth recipes of all sizes get done in nearly the same amount of time using the charcoal amounts in the table. (As long as you are using a standard-depth Dutch oven.) Recipes that are converted by volume instead of by depth will usually get done using the charcoal amounts listed in the table above, but a large batch will take longer than a small batch. If you are doing a really big pot of soup or are cooking in cold weather, you may need to light a second batch of charcoal so your charcoal doesn't go out before you are done cooking.

THE MATH OF CHARCOAL

Since many other reputable sources recommend significantly less charcoal for larger Dutch ovens than I do, I thought it would be good to explain a little of the physics and math behind the numbers I provide. This explanation is over-simplified, but I think it helps one understand the basics of what is going on and why the charcoal amounts in the chart work.

Think for a moment about the food baking inside a Dutch oven. For this example, let's take Cheesy Chicken that is in the ***Bake*** step in an eight-inch Dutch oven. The Cheesy Chicken you are baking has a certain shape—a shape like a flat cylinder. In this case the cylinder is about two inches high and just under eight inches in diameter. Now think about the heat coming toward this cylinder of Cheesy Chicken. It is coming from above and below and could be shown with arrows.

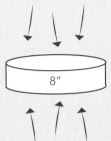

We know that as the heat reaches the Cheesy Chicken from above and below it starts to work its way into the Cheesy Chicken and heat it up. Exactly how it does this is subject to the law of heat diffusion; but how it works its way through doesn't really matter to us at the moment since we know that the amount of heat we have provided for our two-inch-high, eight-inch-diameter Cheesy Chicken will do the job. Now imagine that we have a cylinder of Cheesy Chicken two inches high and just under twelve inches in diameter. In order to find out how much heat we need to apply to this wider cylinder we just have to do a little math. We figure out the surface area of

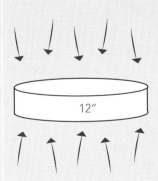

each cylinder (using πr^2) then solve for the relative amount of charcoal needed. Since we already know the amount of charcoal we need for the eight-inch flat cylinder, we can figure out the proportionate amount we need for a twelve inch flat cylinder. The equation looks like this:

X coals/12" area = 16 coals/8" area
X coals = 12" area x 16 coals/8" area
$X = \pi(6 \times 6) \times 16/\pi(4 \times 4)$

The pi's cancel out, 16 divided by 4 x 4 equals 1, and you are left with the number of coals needed for a twelve-inch Dutch oven: 6 x 6 or the radius squared. The same formula works for all the other sizes and in its most basic form works out to be r^2=total coals needed. Too bad all of life isn't that simple!

Lighting a Second Batch of Charcoal

If you are making something that you expect will take extra time, you will need to light a second batch of charcoal to keep it cooking. One way to do this is to bag up a second set of charcoal in advance, dump it out onto a second piece of foil during **Setup**, and build it into a pyramid at the same time you are doing the first set on your lid. When you have completed the **Preheat & Season** step with the first set of coals, light your extra pile. This should make them ready to go about the time that the original coals are dwindling. You can go ahead and leave the original coals on and under the Dutch oven you are cooking in—just add more coals next to them as they become smaller. Charcoal begins to put out noticeably less heat about the time that the coals are half of their original diameter.

In lighting extra coals, keep in mind that when you light charcoal on foil, the ground or other surface under the foil will become much hotter than the ground does when you light charcoal on a lid. Make sure the surface under the foil will not be damaged by the more intense heat.

How Weather Affects Charcoal

When you are cooking out in windy conditions, your charcoal may be more difficult to get started, but the coals will get to the 80 percent gray stage faster once you do get them lit. They will also burn out faster because the wind is providing more air flow. If you think you might need an extra set of coals because of this, plan ahead.

When it is windy, sparks can come off of the coals as you *Light* and as you cook. Although these sparks are small and normally may not do any damage, pay attention to what direction the wind is blowing and what flammable materials may be in the path of the sparks.

If you are cooking in damp conditions, your coals may take longer to *Light* and you may need more matches to get them lit.

If you are cooking in cold conditions, more of the heat from the coals will be lost to the environment. I recommend that you start with the usual amount of coals, but plan that it will take more time and that you will probably need to light a second batch. If the food seems to be cooking too slowly during *Bake*, add extra coals to the lid first. Be careful about putting extra charcoal under the pot, since extra coals under the pot could more easily lead to food burning.

Making Treated "Easy-light" Charcoal

To make treated charcoal for an eight-inch Dutch oven, place 16–18 briquettes in a quart-size heavy duty (freezer weight) zip-seal plastic bag. Pour in ¼ cup (2 ounces) lighter fluid, seal the bag, and rotate it to distribute the lighter fluid. Let it stand ("marinate") at least one hour or overnight. Use within three days or add extra lighter fluid before you use them. For larger Dutch ovens, use a gallon-size heavy duty zip-seal bag. Add 1 ounce of lighter fluid for every 8 coals used. Example: For a ten-inch Dutch oven, use 25 coals and 3 ounces of lighter fluid. Tip: Use a permanent marker to mark ounce lines on a clear plastic disposable cup and use that to measure. Protect your hands with Nitrile or chemical resistant gloves as you measure and pour.

16 coals in a bag   ¼ cup lighter fluid   treated charcoal for an 8" dutch oven

DUTCH OVEN SIZE	8"	10"	12"	14"
Amount of charcoal	16	25	36	49
Amount of lighter fluid	2 oz.	3 oz.	4½ oz.	6 oz.
Size of heavy duty zip-seal bag	quart	gallon	gallon	gallon or 2 gallon

Reusing Extinguished Charcoal

Coals that have been extinguished in the extinguishing bucket can be reused. When the bucket is about 3/4 full, pour in 1 cup lighter fluid, put the lid on tightly, and allow it to sit several hours or overnight.

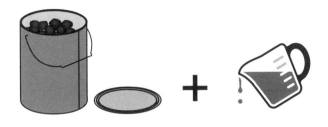

Extinguishing Bucket   1 cup of lighter fluid

This formula assumes you are using a gallon-size new metal paint bucket as your extinguishing bucket. It also assumes that you only have extinguished coals in your bucket, not large amounts of ash.

To use the coals, pour enough coals onto the Dutch oven lid to cover the lid closely in a single layer (see photo). Stack the coals in pyramid-shaped piles and light. Be aware that used coals will light faster but will not last as long. When used with the recipes in this book that bake twenty minutes or less, coals can be reused once.

Since the can will have been tightly sealed, you might want to bring along a straight edge screwdriver or paint-can opener to get the lid open again. Open the lid gently so that you don't end up warping the lid.

Emergency Charcoal Lighting

If you try to light your treated coals and find they won't light, you can light them by using small fire-lighting sticks such as Diamond brand "Strike-a-fire" fire starters. For an eight-inch Dutch oven, arrange the coals and fire starters on the Dutch oven lid as shown with 8 coals grouped around each stick. (Fire starters should be standing on edge. All coals must be touching the sticks.) For larger Dutch ovens, use more lighting sticks, and arrange the coals similarly around each stick. Light both ends of each stick. This method of lighting tends to be a little smoky, but it does work and it is easy to keep emergency lighting sticks in your Dutch Oven Kit until you need them.

COOKING WITH FIRE

You can use a campfire to create coals for Dutch oven cooking, foil cooking or stick cooking. I only recommend trying to use coals from fire for Dutch oven cooking when you feel you are at the "advanced" level or really want a new adventure. I prefer using charcoal with Dutch ovens; however, I often do the main dish part of my meal in the Dutch oven with charcoal, and then do dessert (marshmallows, banana boats—that kind of thing) over coals from a fire. Or, when cooking with kids, I may do foil dinners or hot dogs over the fire, and dessert in a Dutch oven with charcoal.

Contrary to popular belief, fire is not really "hot"—at least it doesn't produce the kind of heat you really need for cooking. Even when roasting marshmallows, the kind of heat you want comes not from the flames, but from the glowing coals that fall down under the flames as the fire burns.

If you want to build a fire that will quickly produce good coals for cooking it can be helpful to know something about types of firewood. Firewood is generally categorized by the terms "tinder," "kindling," and "fuel." (See below). In order to build a fire that will light easily and get going quickly, you will need some firewood of each type. When you build a fire, if you have built your fire well, your match will easily light the tinder. If you have used enough tinder, the tinder will burn long enough to light the kindling. If you have used enough kindling, the kindling will burn long enough to light the fuel.

TYPES OF FIREWOOD

TINDER: Tinder includes small twigs and newspaper. My favorite form of tinder out in nature is "red pine"—twigs or branches where the pine needles have died and turned red.

KINDLING: Kindling includes small branches and finely split logs.

FUEL: Large branches, small logs or large logs that have been split.

There are many possible shapes of fire you can build and each shape has a name. The types I use when I want to build a fire for producing coals are "teepee," "log cabin," and "crisscross." The photos and instructions below will show you how to build your fire using these fire types.

1. Start by building a teepee. Do this off-center in your fire pit so that you will have space to keep the fire going, and space to pull the coals aside for cooking. Use fine tinder at the base of your teepee—material like red pine or paper that will catch fire easily—then add small twigs and build up to larger twigs and small branches. Make your teepee tall and pointed—the height and pointed shape of the teepee will help the fire get going more quickly.

SECTION 4: *The Whys behind the Hows*

2. Before you light your teepee, build a log cabin of small logs around it. Make sure the teepee is large enough that the point comes up through the top of the log cabin (see photo above).

3. Light your tinder. Monitor your fire to make sure it keeps going. Once the log cabin part has caught fire and the teepee has burned down a bit, lay one-to two-inch diameter kindling across the top of the log cabin as if you were building a flat roof onto your log cabin (see photo on following page). This "roof" is the start of a crisscross fire. A crisscross fire is the best fire for generating coals.

4. Continue adding layers of large kindling or small fuel in crisscross style over the top of your log cabin, doing layers going first one direction, and then the other. Add your fuel gradually enough that you don't smother the fire, but steadily enough that the fire has enough "food." In selecting your fuel, keep in mind that smaller diameter pieces will turn into coals more quickly than large logs.

5. Keep the fire going on the side of the fire pit where you started it. Meanwhile, carefully pull coals for cooking from the base of the fire to the other side of the fire pit. (See tips for moving coals below.) As the fire continues to burn, you can pull more coals over as needed. If you will only need the coals for about 20–30 minutes of cooking, you can build a smaller fire and wait for whole fire burn down into coals before using them.

Using your Coals:

STICK COOKING: keep the coals piled up a bit after you pull them out from under the fire. This will result in more intense heat that works well for stick cooking.

FOIL COOKING: if you are cooking food wrapped in foil directly on the coals (for example, foil dinners) pull out only the coals that are fairly small and uniform in size. Spread the coals in an even layer and lay the foil packages directly on the coals. Use a glove to occasionally re-position and check the foil packets. When one side is done, turn them to the other side.

DUTCH OVEN: If you want to use the coals for Dutch oven cooking, you may wish to have a fire proof work surface outside of the fire pit, for example, a metal garbage can lid—this can help you keep track of the ash and coals. You can use a shovel to transfer the coals to your work surface. For the first few Steps, you will want to have all the coals on the Dutch oven lid, under the Dutch oven. For **Bake** you will want move the lid onto the pot and put some new coals under the Dutch oven and some new coals on the lid. Coals that come from hard woods will burn longer and hotter. If you only have soft woods (like pine) it may be difficult for you to get the heat you need and you will need to replace the coals frequently. Hold your hand a few inches above the coals on the lid to gauge the heat coming off of them—you should be able to hold your hand there for about four to five seconds before you have to move it. It is a good idea to rotate the Dutch oven pot with respect to the coals and rotate the lid with respect to the pot every so often to avoid having hot spots affect your food. After you are done with the coals, move them back into the fire pit and extinguish as directed below.

Moving Coals

Moving coals from one part of the fire pit to another is very hot work. You can make the process safer and more comfortable by:

★ Using a long-handled shovel to move the coals

★ Wearing heavy-duty gloves

★ Wearing long sleeves and getting them wet

★ Wearing a wet bandana over your face

★ Pulling your hair back

★ Misting your skin with water before you start

★ Keeping first-aid supplies on hand

Fire Safety Rules

Rules about fire use may vary according to conditions and location. Basic fire safety rules include:

★ Use an established fire-pit away from trees.

★ Keep firewood well away from the fire

★ Always bring enough water to properly extinguish the fire.

★ Keep the fire small and under control

★ Never leave a fire unattended.

★ Check that the fire is completely out and cold to the touch before you leave!

Extinguishing a Fire

Fire can travel underground, even through soil. Protect yourself and the environment by making sure your fire is out cold. Although fire can be smothered with non-organic materials like sand, the most effective and sure way to extinguish a campfire is using water:

★ Don't use logs in your fire that will take longer to burn than you will have at your campfire—it is more difficult to fully extinguish a partially burned log than one that is more completely burned or has burned down to coals.

★ Reduce the heat being produced by your fire by moving burning logs apart from each other and spreading out the coals within the fire pit. Break up partially burned logs as much as possible.

★ Sprinkle the coals with water. Turn the coals. Repeat. If you have a partially burned log, pour water on the log. Wait. Repeat.

★ You are done when the coals/logs stop producing steam or smoke and you can put your hand down flat on the coals or log without sensing heat.

THE TINDER BOX

Up until a couple hundred years ago, it was common to keep a waterproof box with a little bit of tinder in it—material that would catch fire easily even in damp conditions. If you are a camper and have to light a campfire on a regular basis, make your life easier by creating your own "tinder box." Use any kind of waterproof container (even a zip-seal plastic bag) and fill it with your favorite type of fire-starting material. (See also page 178.)

COOKING OVER A BUTANE STOVE

In situations where there are restrictions on the use of charcoal or fire, you can use a butane stove with your eight-inch, ten-inch, or twelve-inch Dutch oven. Please note that some recipes work better than others over a butane burner. Those that work best tend to be the ones that use *Fry/Simmer* and do not use *Bake*. It can also work with recipes such as Cheesy Chicken because it is not layered and can be stirred frequently while it is cooking, or Chicken and Dumplings since the biscuits don't have to bake—they can just steam. The most difficult thing about cooking over a butane stove tends to be that you can only turn it down so far before the flame goes out or blows out. Because of this, it can be difficult to adjust the heat low enough to keep some foods from burning as they cook. A butane stove is best used as an emergency alternative when you can't use charcoal; or when you want to cook a soup or sautéed meal quickly and with minimum bother.

1. Set up the stove. Insert and lock in the fuel can according to the instructions with the stove.

2. Place the oiled Dutch oven over the burner.

3. Light the burner according to the instructions that came with the stove. Note: with most stoves the burner will not light if butane can is not correctly locked in.

4. *Preheat & Season* and *Fry/Simmer* with the heat set to about half to two-thirds of maximum. (If oil starts smoking noticeably during seasoning, it is turned slightly too hot.)

5. For *Bake*, turn the flame as low as you can get it and still have a steady flame.

If the food burns on, clean the pot by simmering water in it until the food loosens, or use a copper scrubbing pad to remove food residue completely, then reseason well the next time you use the Dutch oven. Since you can't bake bread items over a butane stove, and cobblers are hard to do (or don't turn out very well), here are a couple of recipes to use specifically with a Dutch oven and butane burner.

QUESADILLAS

1. Place lid upside-down on burner. Make sure it is centered. If using eight-inch tortillas, use a ten- or twelve-inch lid. If using ten-inch tortillas, use a twelve-inch lid.

2. Light burner and turn to lowest possible setting. Depending on your burner, you will need it on the lowest setting or very close to the lowest setting.

3. Oil the lid and *Preheat & Season*.

4. Swipe the lid again with an oily paper towel and put the tortilla on to cook.

5. Cook first side until lightly browned. You will need to cook it anywhere from 20 seconds to 1½ minutes depending on what your lowest burner setting is. The tortilla will cook more evenly if the heat is less.

6. Flip tortilla and cook second side until lightly browned. This will take a shorter time than the first side did. If desired, you can pierce bubbles with the point of your knife.

MAKING THE QUESADILLA:

1. Do steps one through five above. After you flip the tortilla, only cook it for a very short time.

2. Cook a second tortilla using steps 1–5 above. As soon as you flip the tortilla, spread cheese over the tortilla. Top with the first tortilla.

3. Cook until the cheese melts enough to stick to the bottom tortilla. Flip the quesadilla over and cook until the cheese is fully melted.

4. You can cut the quesadilla into quarters or eighths on the lid using your small knife, or better still, with scissors or kitchen

shears. (It's usually not a great idea to use a knife on your seasoned Dutch oven or lid, but it seems to work okay here.)

5. When you are done cooking, use your scraper to remove any cheese from the lid while it is still warm.

INGREDIENT	8" (1x)	10" (1.5x)	12" (2x)
uncooked flour tortillas—8" or 10"	4 (10") or 6 (8")	8 (10") or 8 (12")	12 (10") or 18 (8")
shredded cheddar	1½ cups (5–6 oz.)	3 cups (10–12 oz.)	4½ cups (15–18 oz.)
SERVES	4	8	12

★ Recipe assumes premade, uncooked tortillas. You can also use pre-cooked tortillas. (It's just that they taste so much better when you cook them fresh!)

★ If you want to cook more than one tortilla or quesadilla at a time and have more than one butane burner, you can use your ten- or twelve-inch pot. Because the bottom of the pot sits higher on the burner than the lid, you will need to set the heat slightly higher (but still low).

PUDDING IN A CONE

1. Set up your butane stove and *Preheat & Season*. Keep the stove at the same temperature and add your evaporated milk and water. The liquid should start to simmer almost immediately.

2. Stir in the pudding mix. Keep stirring constantly with the flat bottom of the spoon scraping the bottom of the pot until the color starts to change (you will get little swirls of darker-colored pudding.)

3. Stir often for the next few minutes. When the pudding starts to bubble and steam, turn off the heat. Continue to stir often until the bubbling stops.

4. Allow the pudding to cool, uncovered in the pot, for 15 to 20 minutes. Stir occasionally to keep a "skin" from forming.

5. Serve the pudding in ice cream cones.

INGREDIENT	8" (1x)	10" (1.5x)	12" (2x)
evaporated milk	5-oz. can	2 (5-oz.) cans	3 (5-oz.) cans
water	2 milk cans or 1¼ cups	4 milk cans or 2½ cups	6 milk cans or 3¾ cups
cook and serve pudding mix	3-oz. box	2 (3-oz.) boxes	3 (3-oz.) boxes
ice cream cones	~6	~12	~18
SERVES	~6	~12	~18

★ Recipe assumes regular-size ice cream cones (not extra large.) Put a few mini-marshmallows in the bottom of each ice cream cone before you serve up (either cake or sugar cones) to keep the pudding from leaking out the bottom.

★ Larger eight-inch recipe—You can use a 4.6-oz. box of pudding mix with a 12-oz. can evaporated milk and one milk can of water to make 8–10 servings.

SECTION 4: *The Whys behind the Hows*

· FUEL SECTION—FAQS ·

★ WHY DO I NEED AN EXTINGUISHING BUCKET?

Many small forest fires and house fires each year are started from improperly extinguished charcoal. Extinguishing charcoal by depriving it of oxygen in an extinguishing bucket is one of the surest ways to put out charcoal, and it also provides an easy way to carry out what you carry in.

★ IS IT IMPORTANT TO SEPARATE THE COALS FROM THE ASHES WHEN EXTINGUISHING? WHY NOT JUST POUR BOTH IN THE EXTINGUISHING BUCKET?

The charcoal will go out faster and retain less heat if you tap the ashes off of the coals before placing them in the extinguishing bucket. Also, if you plan to reuse the charcoal, too much ash in the bucket will soak up all the lighter fluid and prevent the coals from properly "marinating."

★ WHAT ABOUT USING A CHIMNEY STARTER TO LIGHT THE CHARCOAL?

Chimney starters are a very effective way of lighting charcoal, especially non-treated charcoal. A typical chimney starter will have a compartment for placing paper and a compartment for the charcoal. For the method in this book, we have chosen not to recommend the chimney starter for a few reasons:

- It's one more thing to have to carry.

- It takes the same amount of time as the lighting method described in the steps.

- When you light the coals on the lid, it simultaneously preheats and seasons the lid—something you don't get if the charcoal are in a chimney starter.

★ WHAT IF I FORGET TO MARINATE THE COALS AHEAD OF TIME?

You can pile the coals on the lid and spray them with lighter fluid, wait a few minutes, then light them. The coals might be a little slower lighting, but it works okay, as long as you have the lighter fluid with you. If not, you can use emergency lighting sticks (see "Emergency Charcoal Lighting" on page 157). For safety reasons, it is best not to spray lighter fluid on coals that are already partially lit.

★ WHAT ARE THE PROS AND CONS OF USING MATCHLIGHT VERSUS MARINATING MY OWN CHARCOAL?

In terms of cost, there is very little difference. The main advantage of marinating your own has to do with shelf-life. Once a bag of Matchlight is opened, the lighter fluid in the charcoal will begin to evaporate. Charcoal from a bag that has been open a week or two will not light as well. By keeping lighter fluid and charcoal on hand and marinating your own, you can choose to have "freshly marinated" charcoal each time you cook. You can, of course, re-marinate charcoal if the lighter fluid evaporates.

★ WHY DO YOU SAY NOT TO USE CHEAPER BRANDS OF CHARCOAL?

I tested every store brand of charcoal I could find. Many of them seemed to have "raw" (not converted to charcoal) wood chips in them. All of them were harder to light and seemed to not burn as long or as hot. If you decide to test a store brand, try lighting an equal pile of store brand side by side with Kingsford, or another good brand, so you can have a controlled comparison.

★ HOW CAN YOU TELL IF THE CHARCOAL ARE LIGHTING?

As mentioned in the Steps, you can hold your hand above the coals to see if heat is coming off, you can fan the coals to see them glow red, or you can shade them and see the glow as shown in this photo.

★ I MARINATED THE COALS ACCORDING TO THE INSTRUCTIONS, OR I USED MATCHLIGHT CHARCOAL, BUT THEY STILL DIDN'T LIGHT WELL. WHAT WENT WRONG?

Ask yourself the following problem-solving questions:

- Were the coals treated with the right amount of lighter fluid? Was the plastic bag free from holes? Did you use them within a few days of bagging and marinating them?

- If you were using Matchlight, it is possible your bag had a small hole when you purchased it, allowing the lighter fluid to evaporate some before you bought it. If you still have charcoal in the bag, open it and sniff—you should be able to smell the fumes.

- Did you pile the coals in a tall pyramid? Did they get enough oxygen?

- Did you wait until they were gray before using them?

- Was the weather damp? Were the coals exposed to water or a damp climate before they were bagged?

★ YOU RECOMMEND DIVIDING UP THE CHARCOAL INTO PILES OF NO MORE THAN 16 DURING LIGHT. WHAT IS THE REASON FOR THIS?

When lighting 36–38 coals for a twelve-inch or 49–51 coals for a fourteen-inch the coals light better when divided into separate piles. This is what happens: when a large number are in one pile, it seems that the coals on the inside of the pile don't get enough oxygen. Given enough time, they will light, but by the time the interior coals are lit, the outer coals will already be burned partway down and thus will not produce as much heat when spread out. The optimum pile size seems to be between 10 and 16 coals.

When lighting coals for Dutch ovens 10" or larger, separate the coals into smaller piles for more efficient lighting. Shown here—coals lighting on the lid of a 14" Dutch oven.

★ WHY IS IT IMPORTANT TO PILE THE COALS IN A TALL PYRAMID SHAPE (STEP 2)?

The taller the pyramid, the faster the coals light—you can actually measure the difference in time. I don't know enough physics to know exactly why this is, but I assume it has to do with the fact that hot air rises. The same principle seems to be at work when you build a teepee fire—taller, narrower teepees seem to burn better and hotter.

★ WHY DON'T YOU TALK ABOUT STACKING DUTCH OVENS?

It is possible to stack Dutch ovens during **Bake** and thereby save a few briquettes. I generally don't for several reasons:

- It is much harder to check the food when it gets done.

- It is a little trickier to make sure each Dutch oven has just the heat it needs.

- Stacked Dutch ovens are much more susceptible to being influenced by wind.

- If different small groups of people are in charge of different Dutch ovens, it makes the whole process more complicated—and we are going for simple.

- Because I extinguish and reuse my charcoal, I don't feel like a few extra coals are a "waste."

★ **WHY IS IT IMPORTANT NOT TO LEAVE THE COALS LIGHTING TOO LONG ON THE LID?**

Even under normal conditions, it is possible for the intense heat of the coals to burn away part of the seasoning coat on the lid. This isn't really a problem because you can reseason. The real problem is that that kind of intense heat, left in one spot of the lid for a long time, can cause the metal to become denatured. For more information, see "Dutch Oven Rehab," page 98.

★ **I'VE HEARD THAT YOU CAN LIGHT A SECOND BATCH OF CHARCOAL BY PLACING ONE NEW COAL NEXT TO EACH OLD COAL AS THE FOOD BAKES. DOES THAT WORK?**

I've heard that too, but I've never been able to get it to work.

★ **I'VE SEEN A LOT OF CHARTS FOR HOW MUCH CHARCOAL TO USE FOR DIFFERENT SIZES OF DUTCH OVENS AND MOST OF THEM DON'T SEEM SIMILAR TO YOURS. WHY?**

I assume the other charts are based on different types of formulas. All I know is that for the recipes in this book, the formula I use works really well. The same-depth recipe scaled to a different size Dutch oven comes out amazingly similar and in almost exactly the same length of time in a twelve- or fourteen-inch as in an eight-inch—just 2 to 5 minutes longer for the larger Dutch ovens. This slight increase in time may be due to the fact that the twelve- and fourteen-inch Lodge Dutch ovens have three-quarter inches more interior pot depth than a Lodge eight-inch and therefore the coals are about three-quarter inches further from the top of the food.

★ WHAT WOULD HAPPEN IF I USED MORE CHARCOAL THAN RECOMMENDED? OR LESS? WHAT DO I DO IF I NEED WATER TO BOIL AND NOT JUST SIMMER?

When used with *Fry/Simmer* the recommended amount of charcoal brings a liquid to a little below boiling—the liquid will steam and form small bubbles on the bottom, but bubbles will not break the surface. When used with *Bake*, the food will cook in a way that is similar to it cooking in a 350-degree oven. If you need to bring a liquid to a true boil, you would need more charcoal under the Dutch oven, but at some point it becomes difficult to fit more charcoal under the Dutch oven. For boiling water you would be better off using a more efficient heat source such as propane or butane. When baking, you need time for the heat to diffuse into the food. If you use more charcoal, it is likely that the food will burn on the top and bottom before the heat can be adequately transferred into the middle of the food. If you use less charcoal than recommended, it will take longer for the food to cook and you may need to replace the charcoal partway through the cooking process. Using less charcoal during *Bake* would in essence be like baking something in your home oven at 250 or 275 that should be baked at 350 or 375. It takes longer but also can affect the quality of the food.

★ DO YOU HAVE SUGGESTIONS FOR WHAT TO USE IN A "TINDER BOX"?

One of the easiest (and most versatile) things to carry is the type of facial tissue that is treated with lotion—one of these will burn for about a minute. A cotton ball rolled in petroleum jelly will burn for longer than a minute with a clear bright flame.

★ WHAT IS THE BEST WAY TO STORE CHARCOAL? WHAT ABOUT LIGHTER FLUID?

Untreated charcoal can be stored almost indefinitely if it is kept dry. If charcoal is exposed to damp air though, it will soak up the dampness; it becomes "stale" and nearly impossible to light. If you live in a damp area, or plan to store your charcoal in an area that could experience high humidity, I recommend placing your freshly opened charcoal in five-gallon buckets that can be sealed. You may wish to put the coals in sealed bags inside the buckets. Lighter fluid can also be stored for longer periods of time, but it is a good idea to rotate your stock, using up your old as you buy new. Keeping charcoal on hand is a great idea for emergency preparedness, and it allows you to be ready to cook out anytime!

★ **IN STEP 6: EXTINGUISH, YOU SAY TO FOLD THE FOIL AROUND THE ASHES. WON'T THE FOIL BE TOO HOT TO TOUCH WITHOUT GLOVES?**

If you are careful, you can wrap the ashes in the foil without using gloves because even though the ashes are still quite warm, the foil itself will be cool. Just fold the foil together and avoid touching the part with the ashes. If you have gotten holes in your foil, you will probably want to use another sheet of foil around the first one—the less oxygen the ashes have, the quicker they will cool down. Hint: If the weather is cool, the foil packet of ashes can make a very nice hand-warmer.

SECTION 4: The Whys behind the Hows

· PLANNING FOR GROUPS ·

The Step-by-step cookout method was developed with groups in mind—especially youth groups and family groups. Children as young as three or four can safely help with stirring the meat during *Fry* (with appropriate supervision). Slightly older children can mix ingredients in a zip-seal bag or transfer coals to the extinguishing bucket using the tongs. Starting with age ten or eleven, they can follow the Steps and do the easy recipes by themselves, with an adult available to help to light the charcoal and to answer questions and supervise.

If you are a youth leader supervising a group of campers cooking out at the same time, there are a couple approaches you can take to planning the food for your Dutch oven cookout:

APPROACH A: You divide the campers into cooking groups. Each group cooks their own one-pot meal. Leaders who aren't cooking join a group for eating.

PROS: easy to plan and execute.

CONS: if you have large Dutch ovens, you may need to have more people in the group than can realistically help with cooking. Also, it is harder to accommodate picky eaters.

APPROACH B: You divide the campers into cooking groups. Each group cooks a different meal and then serves it as part of a Dutch oven buffet (see page 39 and 43).

PROS: Everyone gets to try everything and it makes it easy to accommodate picky eaters. Three or four people can cook with a large Dutch oven and the food will be shared around.

CONS: Takes a little more planning to make sure the amount of servings being cooked are the amount of servings you will need for the group as a whole.

Approach B is my personal favorite. I have seen it work well over and over again with diverse groups and diverse Dutch oven sizes. In my experience, if you do Approach B, you will need a little more food than you would expect. For a group of 40 people who will be eating, I recommend doing about 16 batches of main dish, appetizer or bread, and about 8 batches of dessert.

The checklists below can help you, whichever approach you choose.

AHEAD OF TIME:

★ Find out how many will be cooking and how many will be eating. You will also need to know how many Dutch ovens you have available and what sizes they are. If desired, you can have the kids or youth who will be cooking look through the recipes and indicate which ones they are most interested in trying.

★ Plan your menu based on the Dutch ovens you have available, the number of cookout groups you want to have, and the total number of people who will need to eat. Ideally you will have no more than three or four campers cooking with one Dutch oven. Use Super-Easy and Easy recipes for beginners. As you select your recipes, keep in mind any special diet needs or preferences members of your group may have (vegetarian, gluten intolerance, and so on).

★ Make sure you will have enough Dutch Oven Kits and extinguishing buckets. Typically three to five groups can share one Dutch Oven Kit (as long as you have extra cooking spoons) and two to three groups can share an extinguishing bucket. Keep in mind that extinguishing buckets fill up faster when using larger Dutch ovens.

★ Create your grocery shopping list. Add up the total amount you need of ingredients that appear in multiple recipes. You may opt to buy items like chicken tenders, ground beef patties, shredded cheddar, butter, or sour cream in bulk and then divide them into smaller bags for the various recipes. When I am creating my shopping list, I like to divide the list the way the Standard Ingredient List is divided—with segments for refrigerated and frozen items, produce, canned goods, dry goods, and seasonings—this makes doing the shopping easier.

★ Do your shopping. I like to buy all the frozen (or freezable) and non-perishable items as much as several weeks in advance. When possible, I have some of the youth help me do the shopping. Once we are in the grocery store, I give one part of the shopping list to each pair of young people. When they bring their items back, we double check them with my master shopping list.

★ Premeasure all your ingredients and prebag your charcoal. Place all the ingredients for a certain recipe in a bag with a copy of the recipe. I usually have a little "bagging party" a few days in advance of the cookout and invite those who will be cooking out to come help divide up the food and charcoal. It usually is a lot of fun.

★ Check the weather forecast a day or two before you will be leaving. If the forecast calls for conditions to be damp, cold, or windy, you may end up having to light an extra batch of coals in order to get your food done. If you think you might need extra coals, you can always bag them at home and then take lighter fluid with you and marinate them at your campsite. Even if the weather doesn't turn bad, having some extra charcoal and lighter fluid with you can help you feel more prepared.

★ Before you leave home, double check that each recipe bag has all the needed ingredients and that you have all the necessary refrigerated and frozen ingredients. This is especially critical if you had a group helping you bag—with lots of people it's easy for an ingredient to go astray, and you really don't want to have to sort this out when you are ready to cook! As harried as you may be before you leave for your cookout, this is worth a little extra time. Also, if you are not using Matchlight, make sure you marinate your charcoal within three days or less of when you plan to use it.

★ Select sites ahead of time—campground, driveway—and figure out where each group should cook.

★ If you have a variety of sizes of Dutch ovens, assign younger campers to groups using smaller size Dutch ovens.

A CASE STUDY

For a recent cookout, I knew I would have around 30 people cooking (youth of various ages and some leaders) and about 40 people eating. I had the following Dutch ovens available: 1 fourteen-inch deep, 2 fourteen-inch, 2 twelve-inch, 1 ten-inch deep, and 4 eight-inch. I had three Dutch Oven Kits and five extinguishing buckets. The cooking groups made the following recipes:

APPETIZER:

• 3x Nacho Cheese Sauce in the ten-inch deep

MAIN DISHES:

• 4x Cheesy Chicken in the fourteen-inch deep (I used extra charcoal to compensate for the extra depth)
• 3x Taco Soup in a twelve-inch
• 3x Lasagna in a twelve-inch—vegetarian version
• 1x Chicken Enchiladas in an eight-inch
• 1x Chicken Enchiladas in an eight-inch
• 1x Cowboy Potatoes in an eight-inch
• 1x Cowboy Potatoes in an eight-inch

DESSERTS:

• 3x Hot Fudge Cake in a fourteen-inch
• 4x Peach Cobbler (with 5x peaches) in a fourteen-inch

As it turned out on this particular night, I had about two batches of Taco Soup left over while most of everything else was eaten. There was one vegetarian in the group and she was happy with the Lasagna, appetizer, and desserts.

AT THE COOKOUT:

★ Give each cooking group a copy of the cookout steps and a recipe. It works well to give each member of the group an assignment. (See "Group Assignments" on page 186.)

★Give each group a Dutch oven, a bag of premeasured ingredients, and a bag of prebagged and treated charcoal. Have your Dutch Oven Kit(s), jug(s) of water and extinguishing bucket(s) centrally located for the cooking groups to use. You can use the photo on page 13 as a visual checklist to make sure you have everything out that you need.

★Demonstrate **Setup** and **Light**. Help all the groups get their charcoal lit, then have each group read the other steps and their recipe while the charcoal is lighting.

★Plan activities to keep kids/youth occupied while the charcoal is lighting. You can also have them read the FAQs in each Step and take the quiz at the end of this section.

★Make sure that charcoal is extinguished, garbage put away, and Dutch Oven Kit equipment tidied up before the food is served. It can be a good idea to wait until all the groups are done cooking before any of the groups start to eat.

★If you are doing a Dutch oven buffet, make a small sign for each recipe. Let the members of the cooking group put their names on the sign that goes with their recipe. When you set up the buffet, set each sign by the dish it goes with so the cooks can get credit for their cooking. When everyone is done eating, transfer leftovers out of the Dutch ovens and have those who cooked in a certain Dutch oven take that same Dutch oven to clean.

GROUP ASSIGNMENTS

It is easier and more fun to learn to cook with your Dutch oven when you cook with someone. When you are learning to cook, 2–3 people per Dutch oven is an ideal number. Below are some suggested job assignments for the members of each cooking group:

READER—(should have a watch) reads the instructions aloud during each step, keeps track of time for each step, and washes and dries the Dutch oven.

RUNNER—arranges and lights the coals, brings equipment as needed from the Dutch Oven Kit and returns it, extinguishes the coals, and makes sure the area is clean.

COOK—checks to see that all items needed for the recipe are there, prepares food, serves food, and scrapes the pot.

Before you start your cookout, use the photo on page 13 to double check that your cooking group has what it needs. When cooking out with a large number of people, 3–5 cooking groups can share one Dutch Oven Kit (as long as there are extra cooking spoons) and 2 cooking groups can share an extinguishing can and gallon jug of water.

LEAVE NO TRACE

When you camp or cook out with large groups out in nature, the kind of impact you will have on your camping area is especially important. The "Leave No Trace" principles outline the basics of keeping nature natural as you camp. The Step-by-Step method supports the principles and goals of Leave No Trace. Read them and follow them. Enough said.

Seven principles of Leave No Trace

1. Plan ahead and prepare.

2. Travel and camp on durable surfaces.

3. Dispose of waste properly.

4. Leave what you find.

5. Minimize campfire impacts.

6. Respect wildfire.

7. Be considerate of other visitors.

Some specific guidelines from the Leave No Trace program:

★ Know the regulations and special concerns for the area you'll visit.

★ Prepare for extreme weather, hazards, and emergencies.

★ Repackage food to minimize waste.

★ Pack it in, pack it out—pack out all trash, leftover food and litter.

★ To wash yourself or your dishes, carry water 200 feet away from streams or lakes and use small amounts of biodegradable soap.

★ Leave rocks, plants, and other natural objects as you find them.

★ Never feed animals. Feeding wildlife damages their health, alters natural behaviors, and exposes them to predators and other dangers. Store food securely and keep garbage and food scraps away from animals so they will not acquire bad habits. Help keep wildlife wild.

★ Respect other visitors and protect the quality of their experience.

★ Let nature's sounds prevail. Keep the noise down and leave radios, tape players and pets at home.

COOKOUT STEPS QUIZ

1. NAME one reason to preheat.

2. NAME one reason to season.

3. WHERE should the coals be when you are *Frying*?

4. HOW can you tell if the coals are still lighting (haven't gone out)?

5. WHY is it important to cover the extinguishing bucket?

6. WHICH step of Dutch oven cooking sanitizes the Dutch oven?

EXTRA CREDIT: name all the cookout steps in order.

Conclusion

• •

I often compare the recipes in this book to the songs in a beginning guitar book. In a beginning guitar book, the songs aren't there just because they are nice songs but because they will help you learn the method. As you practice those beginning songs, you start to get a feel for how it all works. You begin to know some things by heart and you get ideas for how to use the chords and techniques you have learned to play your favorite songs or make up your own.

It is my hope that this book will do that for you. I believe that by learning the science and practicing the Steps, you will be able to quickly move beyond being a beginner. The recipes in this book will always come in handy because they are easy (and yummy) and scaled to different sizes, but once you have the Steps down, I hope you will also go beyond the recipes in this book to do some more advanced Dutch oven cooking.

Here are some ideas for where to go from here:

★ Make up a new recipe using the Standard Ingredient List (that's how my niece invented Kara's Razzmatazz).

★ Figure out how to do one of your favorite family recipes in your Dutch oven.

★ Explore other Dutch oven books. I especially recommend *Best of the Black Pot* by Mark Hansen and *Black Pot for Beginners.*

Mark's recipes are primarily from-scratch and he gives a great deal of detail, in essence walking you "step-by-step" through what you need to do. In both books he teaches cooking skills applied to Dutch oven dishes and encourages you to experiment.

★ "Like" Dutch Oven Cookout on Facebook. Share your photos and comments with others.

If you are looking for more ideas for ways to cook while camping, I suggest starting with the camping "bible"—*Roughing It Easy* by Dian Thomas. First published in 1974, this book has already influenced two generations of campers and contains a huge number of camping ideas. If you are looking for more help in organizing a camping trip for youth (specifically girls) I recommend Stephanie Worlton's book *Everything You Need to Know about Girls Camp: the Essential Planning Guide for Leaders.*

Last but not least, I encourage you to visit my webpage and blog for:

★ Updates on recipes I'm testing

★ More helps on planning for groups

★ Other Dutch oven hints

Although I love Dutch oven, I also have lots of other interests, including international recipes and travel. I'll be writing about all these things on my blog! **WWW.MICHELEPIKANIELSON.COM**

LIST OF FAQS

1. Everyone talks about seasoning a Dutch oven. What does that mean? Page 105

2. What does the seasoning coat do for the Dutch oven? Why is it important? Page 105

3. Why is it important to preheat the Dutch oven? Page 105

4. I have a brand new Dutch oven. Do I need to do anything to it before I use it? Page 106

5. How do different brands of Dutch ovens compare? Page 106

6. I want to label my Dutch oven so it doesn't get mixed up with others. Is there a good way to do this? Page 107

7. You recommend using the eight-inch size. What are the pros and cons of the other sizes? Page 108

8. Some people I know line their Dutch oven with foil before cooking in it. Should I do that? Page 109

9. What happens if I apply too much oil when seasoning a Dutch oven? Page 110

10. Some people say it is better to use shortening for seasoning a Dutch oven and some prefer oil. Is there a reason to use one or the other? Page 110

11. Is there a type of oil that is better to use? Page 111

12. Do I need to season the Dutch oven after I clean it? Page 111

13. I've heard you should always oil the Dutch oven after you use it. Is that true? Page 112

14. I've heard that you should oil the Dutch oven before you put it away and that as long as you use just a thin coating of oil it shouldn't go rancid during storage. Is this true? Page 112

15. Why do most other books say to oil the Dutch oven before putting it away? Page 113

16. If I am going to be storing my Dutch oven for a few months, is there anything special I should do before putting it away? Page 113

17. Can I use an indoor Dutch oven for outdoor cooking? Can I use my camping Dutch oven for indoor cooking? Page 114

18. I got an old Dutch oven at a yard sale. How do I make it ready to use? Page 114

19. I've heard that you should never pour cold water into a hot Dutch oven. Is that true? Page 114

20. I've heard I should never use soap in my Dutch oven. Why does this method say it is ok? Page 115

21. I've heard it's not good to use water in a Dutch oven. Is it okay to use water? Why? Page 115

22. I've heard you can clean your Dutch oven with salt and oil or sand and water. What about these methods? Page 116

23. What about using fire to burn out the Dutch oven after use? Page 116

24. What should I do if I have problems getting the Dutch oven clean? Page 117

25. Should I do anything different when I clean my Dutch oven indoors? Page 117

26. What if something happens, and I don't get a chance to clean the Dutch oven right away? Page 118

27. I've heard you should never put a Dutch oven in a dishwasher. What happens if you do? Page 118

28. Do I need to clean the Dutch oven every time I use it? Page 118

29. It seems like I am using a lot of paper towels? Is there anything I can do to minimize that? Page 119

30. What is the purpose of the Standard Ingredient List? Page 144

31. In some of the recipes the twelve-inch version is 2x and in some it is 3x. Why is that? Page 144

32. I've heard Dutch ovens will absorb flavors from food or soap and pass those flavors on. Should I worry about that? Page 145

33. I've heard that cooking acidic foods in a Dutch oven can be problematic. What's the scoop on that? Page 145

34. I accidentally stirred the cake mix into the fruit when I was making cobbler. What can I do? Page 146

35. Can I substitute regular milk for evaporated milk in the recipes? Page 146

36. Can I substitute canned chicken for frozen chicken in the recipes? Page 146

37. I followed the instructions but my recipe is brown on top but too gooey still in the middle. What should I do? Page 147

38. I made a batch of cornbread and it wasn't all eaten. Can I keep it in the Dutch oven overnight and eat it for breakfast? Page 147

39. I only have an extra-deep Dutch oven in the size I want to use. Can I still make same-depth recipes? Page 148

40. Do Crock-pot recipes convert well for use in a Dutch oven? Page 148

41. Why do I need an extinguishing bucket? Page 170

42. Is it important to separate the coals from the ashes when extinguishing? Why not just pour both in the extinguishing bucket? Page 170

43. What about using a chimney starter to light the charcoal? Page 171

44. What if I forget to marinate the coals ahead of time? Page 171

45. What are the pros and cons of using Matchlight versus marinating my own charcoal? Page 172

46. Why do you say not to use cheaper brands of charcoal? Page 172

47. How can you tell if the charcoal are lighting? Page 173

48. I marinated the coals according to the instructions or I used Matchlight charcoal, but they still didn't light well. What went wrong? Page 173

49. You recommend dividing up the charcoal into piles of no more than 16 during Light. What is the reason for this? Page 174

50. Why is it important to pile the coals in a tall pyramid shape (Step 2)? Page 175

51. Why don't you talk about stacking Dutch ovens? Page 175

52. Why is it important not to leave the coals lighting too long on the lid? Page 176

53. I've heard that you can light a second batch of charcoal by placing one new coal next to each old coal as the food bakes. Does that work? Page 176

54. I've seen a lot of charts for how much charcoal to use for different sizes of Dutch ovens and most of them don't seem similar to yours. Why? Page 177

55. What would happen if I used more charcoal than recommended? Or less? What do I do if I need water to boil and not just simmer? Page 177

56. Do you have suggestions for what to use in a "tinder box"? Page 178

57. What is the best way to store charcoal? What about lighter fluid? Page 178

58. In Step 6: Extinguish and Eat you say to wrap the foil around the ashes. Won't the foil be too hot to touch without gloves? Page 179

INDEX

A

acidic foods 145
altitude 41
ash brush 33, 127, 128

B

Bake (Step 5) 31
Bake FAQs 32
blog 7,191
brownie analogy 143
buffet - see *Dutch Oven Buffet*
butane stove 165–69

C

can opener 123,128
can sizes 41
Caramel Apple Cobbler 85
charcoal
    amount needed 41,150,176–
        77
    brand 149, 172
    bagging 17,149
    easy-light 17, 149, 154
    emergency lighting 157
    "extra" charcoal 150
    extinguishing 18,33–34, 170
    general info 149
    lighting (see also *Light*) 26,

173, 176
    marinating (see also char-
        coal, easy-light) 154, 171,
        172, 173
    Matchlight - see *charcoal,
    easy-light*
    new batch/second batch 153
    pretreated - see *charcoal,
        easy-light*
    re-using 155
    storing 178
charcoal bucket - see *extinguish-
    ing can*
chimney starter 171
Cheesy Chicken 10, 42 50
Chicken & Broccoli 51
Chicken & Dumplings 74
Chicken Enchiladas 62
Chicken Spanish Rice 42, 63
children - (using Dutch Oven
    Cookout with kids) 180
Clean (Step 7) 35
Clean FAQs 36
cleaning Dutch ovens 111,115–
    20
Cobbler 70, 146
cooking group assignments 186
cooking indoors 114, 117, 137
cone, fir, or spruce 36, 123

converting recipes - see *recipes, converting/scaling*
Corn Chowder 52
Cornbread 42, 59
Cowboy Potatoes 53
Crock-pot 148

D

depth, how it affects recipes-see *recipes, same-depth*
depth, Dutch ovens - see *Dutch ovens, depth comparison and Dutch Ovens, extra-deep*
Dessert Pizza 86
Dutch Oven Buffet 39, 43
Dutch Oven Kit 15, 121–30
Dutch Oven Kit - cleaning 128
Dutch ovens 14, 93
    brands 106–7
    Cleaning FAQs 115
    definition 93
    depth comparison 94, 140, 142
    eight-inch advantages 14, 93
    extra-deep 94, 141–42, 148
    General FAQs 105
    indoor use 114, 117, 137
    labeling 107
    new 14, 106
    preseasoned 14, 95, 106
    rehab 95–99, 114
    season/seasoning 6, 14, 28, 99–104, 105, 106

selecting size 14, 108
stacking 175
storing 113

E

easy-light charcoal - see *charcoal, easy-light*
emergency lighting sticks 127, 157
Enchiladas 64
extinguishing charcoal - see *charcoal, extinguishing*
Extinguish & Eat (Step 6) 33
Extinguish FAQs 34
extinguishing can/bucket 18, 33–34, 127, 170
evaporated milk, using in the recipes 41, 146

F

Facebook 7, 191
Fajitas 76
fire, cooking with 157–65
foil 24, 109, 125, 179
food 16, 131
    bagging 16, 182–83
    Is it done? 32, 147
    storing, transporting 16, 133
    FAQs 144
    food safety 132–35, 147
Fourth of July Cake 60, 141
Fry/Simmer (Step 4) 29
Fuel FAQs 170

fuel 17, 149

G

garbage bags 127
Garden Skillet 78
gloves 126, 128
groups
    assignments 186
    checklists 181
    planning 180
    quiz 189
"gunk" 97

H

HACCP 131
Hamburger Soup 65
hammer 125, 128
Hearty Breakfast 54
Hot Fudge Cake 87

I

ingredient list - see *Standard Ingredient List*

K

Kara's Razzmatazz 42, 68

L

Lasagna 80
Leave No Trace 187–88
Light (Step 2) 25
Light FAQs 26
liquids in Dutch Oven Kit 122

liquids in recipes 40

M

marinating - see *charcoal, easy-light*
matches 38,124, 154
Math of Charcoal 151
menu planning & menus 42
Measurement Conversions 43

N

Nacho Cheese Sauce 42, 55

O

oil 24, 99, 112, 113, 122
    how much 100, 110
    what kind 110, 111, 122
Oriental Fried Rice 66

P

paper towels 119, 126
Parmesan Pull-aparts 69
Peach Cobbler 42, 70
pine cone - see *cone, fir or spruce*
pine needles 37
pot scraper - see *scrape, scraper*
preheat 27–28, 105
Preheat & Season (Step 3) 27
Preheat & Season FAQs 28
Pudding In a Cone 169
pyramid(s) 26, 153, 174–75

Q

Quesadillas 167
Quiz 189

R

rain 38
Ranch Chicken 82
rancid 112
recipes
  converting/scaling 40,
    135–42, 144
  Easy 61
  for butane stove 167–69
  how to use 40
  ingredients list - see *Stan-
    dard Ingredient List*
  ingredient substitution 146
  Intermediate 73
  maximum volume conversion
    141
  regular kitchen use of 135
  same-depth 140
  Super-Easy 49
  Table of Contents 39
Rolls 88
rust 11, 36, 38, 96, 116, 118, 147

S

salt and oil cleaning 116
same-depth recipes - see *recipes, same-depth*
scrape/scraper 36, 123

seasoning - see *Dutch oven,
  season/seasoning*
Setup (Step 1) 23
Setup FAQs 24
Shepherd's Pie 67
shopping, shopping list 144, 182
soap, use with Dutch ovens
  35–36, 100, 115, 122
spoons 35, 121, 128
Standard Ingredient List 40, 44,
  144
Sticky Buns 72
Stir Fry with Rice 83

T

Taco Soup 56
time, for cookout 19, 41
tinder box 165, 178
Tomato Basil Soup 58
tool box (see also Dutch Oven
  Kit) 121
Tortellini Soup 84

W

water 17, 35, 36, 115
weather (affecting charcoal) 32,
  38, 154

Z

zip-seal bags 18, 40, 124, 149,
  154, 180

ABOUT
THE
AUTHOR

Michele Pika Nielson grew up in a house across the street from the University of Utah. As the daughter of two scientists she learned early to apply scientific research methods to all aspects of learning. Since completing her Master's Degree in Language Teaching at the University of Utah, Michele has worked as a teacher, a professional organizer, a cook, a wedding planner, and a flower arranger - among other things. She loves learning languages, developing new recipes, traveling, and working with power tools.

She currently lives with her husband Paul in a little house surrounded by trees in the Millcreek area of Salt Lake City.

0 26575 11343 3